COLUMBIA DOCUMENTS
OF ARCHITECTURE
AND THEORY

COLUMBIA
ARCHITECTURE
PLANNING
PRESERVATION

VOLUME SIX

cba   D.A.P.

SUBSCRIPTION SERVICE
All orders, inquiries, address changes, etc., should be addressed to:

Graduate School of Architecture, Planning and Preservation
Publications Office
403 Avery Hall
Columbia University
New York, NY 10027

Each issue: $15
Subscription prices in U.S.A.: $30 Individual; $50 Institution; $25 Student (with valid ID)
Subscriptions outside the U.S.A.: add $20 for postage and handling

PERMISSIONS AND REPRINTS
For information on permission to quote, reprint or translate *Columbia Documents* material, please write:

D: Columbia Documents of Architecture and Theory
Permissions Department
403 Avery Hall
Columbia University
New York, NY 10027

MANUSCRIPTS
Please address all manuscripts and editorial correspondence to:

The Editor
D: Columbia Documents of Architecture and Theory
403 Avery Hall
Columbia University
New York, NY 10027
Telephone: (212) 854-5885
Fax: (212) 864-0410

Unsolicited manuscripts will be returned only if accompanied by a self-addressed, stamped envelope.

POSTMASTER
Please send address changes to:

Graduate School of Architecture, Planning and Preservation
Publications Office
403 Avery Hall
Columbia University
New York, NY 10027

Columbia Documents of Architecture and Theory (*D*) is published two times a year at Columbia University Graduate School of Architecture, Planning and Preservation.

D: Columbia Documents of Architecture and Theory, Volume Six, 1997.

Copyright © 1997 by the Trustees of Columbia University in the City of New York.

ISBN 1-883584-07-8
ISSN 1065-304X

First published in the United States of America in 1997 by Columbia University Graduate School of Architecture, Planning and Preservation.

Distribution: Distributed Art Publishers

Printed in the United States

Bernard Tschumi: *General Editor*
Stephen Perrella: *Managing Editor/Designer*
Stephanie Salomon: *Copy Editor*
Christopher Perry: *Assistant to the Editors*

EDITORIAL BOARD
Stanley Allen
Rosalyn Deutsche
Arata Isozaki
Kunio Kudo
Catherine Ingraham
Joan Ockman
Stephen Perrella
John Rajchman
Bernard Tschumi

The publication of *D* is sponsored by TOTO Ltd.

CONTENTS   VOL. SIX

5 LIGHT CONSTRUCTION SYMPOSIUM

TERENCE RILEY, MARK TAYLOR, HUGH DUTTON, EEVA-LIISA PELKONEN, GUY NORDENSON,

K. MICHAEL HAYS, GREG LYNN, TOYO ITO AND JOAN OCKMAN

53 JEAN NOUVEL—CARTIER FOUNDATION

71 JACQUES HERZOG AND PIERRE DE MEURON—PROJECTS

79 EMERGING COMPLEXITIES SYMPOSIUM—AKIRA ASADA, SANFORD KWINTER,

ANDREW BENJAMIN AND KUNIICHI UNO

107 PETER EISENMAN—CRITICAL ARCHITECTURE IN A GEOPOLITICAL WORLD

121 WILLIAM MACDONALD AND SULAN KOLATAN—RECENT WORK

157 JESSE REISER AND NANAKO UMEMOTO—RECENT WORK

INTRODUCTION

During the course of a year, many significant exhibitions, lectures and conferences take place at Columbia University's Graduate School of Architecture, Planning and Preservation. The School attempts to present today's most provocative work through "events" by world-class figures. These events extend current debates on the changing nature of architecture and our society, exposing material that may prove useful in dealing with the cultural complexities facing contemporary designers.

Columbia Documents of Architecture and Theory compiles selected material from the lectures and conferences that have taken place recently at the School. Called *D* for short, *Documents* presents work by today's leading theorists and practitioners while questioning the context in which the practice of architecture occurs. Its mandate—to explore architecture's engagement with culture and history—is developed in two issues annually.

EDITORIAL NOTE

The process of compiling the contents of this volume of *Documents*, has made evident a significant transformation in recent architectural thought and practice. The tenets of light construction, as an international sampling of built work, were gathered in an exhibition by the same name, organized by Terence Riley, as an attempt to identify a coherent, new trend in building practices. The various strategies demonstrated in the exhibition suggest a general shift away from instrumental transparency (as in the use of glass) and mere functionalism toward more introspective, self-investigating dematerializations of form. Thus, both technological and metaphorical achievements in the work shown in "Light Construction" register new surface effects and refractive opacities in the architectural facade-as-boundary, or limit condition.

Light construction then, seems to be preparatory, perhaps for the problematizations raised in the second section of this issue of *Documents* beginning with "Emerging Complexities." Certain developments following lightness then, may be seen as an emergent complexity latent *within* architecture. The juxtaposition of the work in "Light Construction" with the apparent topological, temporal and technological characteristics of the latter work in this volume, while indicating new architectural directions, also calls for an inquiry into their interrelations, as they are not mutually exclusive.

LIGHT CONSTRUCTION SYMPOSIUM

TERENCE RILEY, MARK TAYLOR, HUGH DUTTON,

EEVA-LIISA PELKONEN, GUY NORDENSON,

K. MICHAEL HAYS, GREG LYNN, TOYO ITO,

AND JOAN OCKMAN

Panelists in the Light Construction Symposium: Left to right, Kenneth Frampton, Mark Taylor, Greg Lynn, K. Michael Hays, Jacques Herzog, Iñaki Abalos, Juan Herreros, and Joan Ockman.

The School sponsored a symposium in conjunction with The Museum of Modern Art exhibition "Light Construction" on September 22, 1995 in Wood Auditorium. The following is an excerpt from Bernard Tschumi's introduction.

"Light construction" is simultaneously about vision and construction. In the last decade, significant investigations in psychoanalysis, the visual arts and cinema studies have examined our inherited paradigm of vision, putting into question our common view of a self-possessing subject who sees. We are not dealing here with a simple subjectivity, or with a visual perspective. In a corresponding manner, we might say that certain new modes of architecture that increasingly focus on a vocabulary of glass and screens are a way of problematizing representation as well as our assumptions regarding structure. Glass, in light construction, might become a medium to think through these new relationships to structure. Another dimension of light construction is, of course, construction, and more precisely, the role of the construction industry in the making of architecture. In many ways, all of us who build, or who try to build in America, are confronted with this reality. Do we, as architects, determine how things are constructed, as we see in many of the examples shown in the MoMA exhibition, or do we conform to the standards and habits of a very conservative regional and building manufacturing industry? Today architecture could very well be at a juncture between a new understanding of visuality and a new approach to construction technology.

TERENCE RILEY

As the curator of the exhibition "Light Construction," I have probably been given enough opportunity to talk and write about the topic. The one substantial addition I can make is to comment on the background of the show, to provide a personal dimension to its development, that is, how I got to the point where "Light Construction" came to be hanging in the galleries.

First, I would like to change the most likely perceptions that may exist of my relationship to the work exhibited. I feel uncomfortable being perceived as some sort of ambassador from a powerful cultural institution, with little attachment to architecture other than a lofty critical stance. Before working at The Museum of Modern Art or at the Columbia Architecture Galleries, I was in private practice with John Keenen, who also graduated from Columbia's Graduate School of Architecture, Planning and

Preservation. While my position at The Museum of Modern Art may be higher in profile, the practice of architecture has always been a very important part of my life.

Group: Kaakko, Lane, Liimatainen and Tirkkonen: Leisure Studio, Espoo, Finland, 1992.

I'd like to describe how "Light Construction" emerged out of, and away from, what had been personal architectural explorations. My first thoughts on an exhibition about contemporary architecture were very much related to the work I was producing with Keenen; my working title was "Architectonics." Essentially this was going to be a show that would collate buildings related along architectonic lines. I separated buildings according to materials as a way of looking at them, and I noticed that this approach worked for metal, wood, fabric and so on. But the projects I was considering that been constructed out of glass seemed somehow resistant to being characterized strictly by material. They really consisted of an anti-material—one with no fixed character—a somewhat empty image. It was a material that wanted to be something that it couldn't necessarily be by itself. At that point, I renamed the exhibition, focusing on the glass projects, and for a while was referring to it as "Transparencies."

The first notion that sparked the transformation from "Architectonics" to "Transparencies" was, of course, an interest in the simultaneous immateriality and materiality of glass. The reason for the plural, "transparencies," was the realization that the term "transparency" typically had had a singular definition in the modern period: it was the inverse of opacity. There was one absolute sense of transparency. What I found happening today was that there was an architecture that was somewhat recognizable in terms of its forms and its intentions, which appear to recall the language of high modernism, but that there was no longer a conception of transparency as simply the opposite of opaque. That's when the exhibition acquired the name "Transparencies." But even "Transparencies," which I wrote about in ANY just about a year ago, was rather limiting.

Philip Johnson: Ghost House, New Canaan, Connecticut, 1985.

In that article I was investigating certain visual phenomena that were still wholly related to the physical condition of glass. The critical changes in my research had to do with understanding "light construction's" cultural rather than physical qualities. Those cultural dimensions are extremely varied: philosophy, history, physics and so on. I need to admit first and foremost that I'm neither a philosopher nor an historian. This approach implies a certain intellectual promiscuity, yet I think it is the sort of approach most suited to the polyvalent meanings to be read into "light construction."

One of the historical studies that influenced me, in terms of going from "transparencies" to "light construction," was Rosemarie Haag Bletter's essay "Glass Dream," in which she lays out a two-thousand-year history of the search for a transparent architecture, starting with the apocryphal temple of King Solomon, which reportedly had highly polished floors, so

Terence Riley

polished that a visitor would feel as if he were falling through the floor as the light was reflected from it. Bletter traces a whole tradition that includes Mozarabic glass fountains, glass domes that were transformed into Gothic cathedrals and the Parsifal legends—with the image of the grail as a glowing crystal. Bletter's rendering of this incredible history continues through Bruno Taut, who associates glass architecture with the spiritual, the transcendent—both personal transformation and societal transformation. Bletter's historical thread extends into the 1930s in the work of Ludwig Hilberseimer and the Functionalists; a poignant quotation of Hilberseimer refers to the Crystal Palace and its foretelling of rooms of "shadowless light."

Contemporary ideas regarding transparencies are part of this historical continuum and are as culturally derived as those discussed previously. The Swiss literary critic Jean Starobinski touches on many of the contemporary issues surrounding transparency in his essay "Poppaea's Veil." Poppaea was a mistress of the emperor Nero who, with a number of other women, was vying for the emperor's attention. To distinguish herself from her competitors, she adopted the strategy of wearing a veil. The thesis is that the insertion of the veil, the presence of the thing between, sets up a certain subjective relationship between the viewer and the object; a very different relationship from the objective notion of vision implied by the classic modernist glass house, which opens up, expanding to the horizon, suggesting a continuum between the viewer and the world.

Unlike the notion of absolute transparency is one of mediated transparencies, establishing a totally different kind of relationship, a visual relation-

Renzo Piano Building Workshop: Kansai International Airport, Osaka, Japan, 1994.

ship that in French, Starobinski points out, is more properly called a "gaze." I found the etymology of the word quite interesting for its potential link to the architecture in "Light Construction." Whereas vision has very well-known limits and very well-known associations, "to gaze" in French is *regarder*, which comes from root words that mean "to safeguard," to "protect."

In a similar vein, many of the projects that are made out of fencing display a resonance with safeguarding, but with the idea of a veil—putting something between someone and something else. Bernard Tschumi summarized earlier what is at the heart of this whole issue: a definite and very important shift in terms of meaning is occurring from the form of the object to its skin. In reading through some of Hubert Damisch's work it is instructive to note his ideas about perspectival vision and how, it creates form. Like Starobinski, he questions the certitude that has been coupled with form through this particular conception of vision.

What is interesting about Starobinski is that he also comes back to something he calls the reflexive gaze in which, in his words, the world is not all smoke and mirrors, but in which there is the possibility of oscillating between the wisdom associated with vision and the "real" world while protecting the less rationally defined world the senses reveal. So it's neither a clear endorsement one way or the other; it's actually a very common-sense sort of attitude: accepting the kind of wisdom associated with vision and its various benefits, without allowing that vision to overcome or overpower the notion of a different way of seeing or a different way of thinking.

The repeated use of the terms "light" and "lightness" in recent critical and popular publications demonstrates the importance of the root "light"

Nicholas Grimshaw and Partners: Waterloo International Terminal, London, 1993.

Georges Braque: *Violin:*
Mozart /Kubelick, Paris, 1912.

Frank O. Gehry: Frederick R. Weisman
Art Museum, Minneapolis, 1993.

as a key word in contemporary architectural discussions: light, lightness, lightweight. John Rajchman's important reading of Italo Calvino's essay "Lightness" permanently put the word into the consciousness of architects. In a parallel use of the term Renzo Piano used "light," to describe his Kansai International Airport, built on a man-made island. When he first went to see the site, there was none, as it hadn't been built yet. The island was to be made out of "soup" and then transformed into something as hard as possible. Then, a not only incredibly lightweight, but lightly conceived structure was set down on it, with the architect knowing full well that the building would sink and continue to sink for fifty years. When the surveyors went to stake out the building, the contractors had to proceed with work immediately, as the stakes in the ground on the island would begin to move and they would no longer be in relationship with each other as the island shifted and settled. This is an architecture that has no terra firma. This is an architecture that is conceived as existing in a moving matrix. And it does so in an incredibly elegant and important way.

Calvino's forecast for the millennium, in which "lightness" will be a key word, is becoming evident all around us. For architecture it will no doubt play the same important role that the word "constructive" played in the earlier part of this century, during the Machine Age. "Construct," "construction," and "constructivist" all possessed a root concept that did not need to be defined at that time. It was so essential, it pervaded everything. Similarly, "light" is one of those words that is so pervasive it almost absorbs its own meanings. "Light construction" is an intersection of the two key words of the architecture of our time, an architecture that is increasingly drawn to the light, even as it is still tethered, for the time being, to the mechanical world of the early part of this century.

I've said a number of times recently that "light construction" is not an "ism." (The last thing that the twentieth century needs in its final five years is the introduction of a movement.) Nor is it a beauty contest. And maybe the world is not innocent enough anymore to believe this, but there are no architects in the show, only buildings. It's not an attempt to resolve those various issues that a museum exhibition cannot well resolve. It's an attempt to capture a moment in which what was is ceasing to be even as it only seems to know what it wants to become. It's also very good architecture. "Light Construction" represents an architecture at a moment of enormous transference. What appears to be happening now is that architects are absorbing, both literally and sometimes by osmosis, much of the computer world: a world where, in Calvino's words, the iron machines still exist but now are controlled by weightless bits.

Henry-Russell Hitchcock was one of the first American historians to write about modern architecture. He did so most articulately in a very thoughtful, very literate, very well-developed book called *Modern Architecture*.

Alfred Barr, the first director of The Museum of Modern Art, reviewed it and though he generally praised it, spent much of his review telling Hitchcock to be more definitively critical, to cut out who's out and to bring in who's in. The result was that Hitchcock rewrote the book with Philip Johnson as *The International Style*, with its famous three rules regarding volume, regularity and lack of ornament. At this point in time, as Le Corbusier's idealized concept of Mediterranean sunlight recedes, so too, do the forms upon which that light played so magnificently. The flicker of a new light reveals less defined forms. The question remains: is the old set of rules being replaced by a new set, or are the new rules as vague as the new forms?

It was quite discouraging this morning to read that the *New York Times*'s architecture critic believes so strongly in the former. It seems to me that today's new forms are developing quite well without a defined set of rules. Is it really the exhibition curator's task to create a path where none is necessary? After reading Herbert Muschamp's review of "Light Construction," I picked up the section containing the book review and read the first paragraph, which I found to be an interesting rebuttal to Muschamp's arguments regarding the importance of style. I'm speaking of a review by Christopher Lehmann-Haupt of Milan Kundera's new book of essays in which he notes: "One of the main points Kundera insists on most strenuously in his stimulating new non-fiction work is Nietzsche's injunction that we should neither corrupt the actual way our thoughts come to us nor, in Kundera's paraphrase, should we turn our ideas into systems." That's not a completely unproblematic idea, and I'm aware that we live in a problematic time. However, I do believe ours is a time unlike Hitchcock's and Johnson's: we should resist the impulse to make a new set of three rules, resist the impulse to make new systems.

I'd like to read a few lines from the play *Angels in America* by Tony Kushner. The words of the character Alexi Antediluvianovich Prelapserianoff, "the world's oldest living Bolshevik," point to some of the issues I've spoken about, issues that define our transitional times: "And Theory, how are we to proceed without Theory. What System of Thought have these reformers to present to this mad swirling planetary disorganization, to this evident welter of fact, events, phenomena, calamity?" Having previously referred to his countrymen as vipers, he continues, "If a snake sheds his skin before a new skin is ready, naked he will be in the world, prey to the forces of chaos. Have you, my little serpents, a new skin?" In Kushner's play, Prelapserianoff speaks of the need for theory and uses "the skin" as its metaphor. In "Light Construction," I have considered architecture's skin, looking to it not as a metaphor for a new architectural theory but as its herald.

Terence Riley studied architecture at the University of Notre Dame and Columbia University. Since 1984 he has been in private practice with John Keenan. Keenan/Riley's work has been published and exhibited widely. In addition to their design work, both partners have been involved in teaching and speaking in the United States and Europe.

In 1989, Riley curated, "Paul Nelson: Filter of Reason," the inaugural exhibition at the Arthur Ross Architecture Galleries at Columbia University. He also directed an exhibition on the work of Iacov Chernikhov and a restaging of MoMA's first exhibition on architecture entitled "Exhibition 15: the International Style and The Museum of Modern Art." He has been an adjunct faculty member since 1987.

Riley joined MoMA in October 1991 and was appointed Chief Curator in September of 1992. He has curated six shows at MoMA, including exhibitions on Bernard Tschumi, Rem Koolhaas and Frank Lloyd Wright, which was the most comprehensive retrospective presentation of his architectural work since his death in 1959. His most recent show, "Light Construction," a survey of contemporary architecture, is currently on exhibit at the Museum of Contemporary Art in Barcelona.

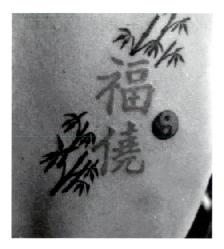

Left: Kenneth Frampton;
right: Mark C. Taylor.

REFLECTIONS ON SKIN

> Oh, those Greeks! They knew
> how to live. What is required for
> that is to stop courageously at the
> surface, the fold, the skin, to
> adore appearance, to believe in
> forms, tones, words, in the whole
> Olympus of appearance. Those
> Greeks were superficial—*out of
> profundity.*
>
> —Nietzsche

> The deepest thing in man
> is his skin.
>
> —Paul Valéry

Skin. Surface. What is so deep about
skin? What is so profound about
surface? What is so superficial about
profundity?

Though it seems obvious, it is no
longer clear … clear that we know
what surface is. Nor is skin any longer
transparent. We must, therefore,
begin by asking about the point at
which we all begin … and end: the
skin. What is skin? As is always the
case, the positive emerges through the
negative, and vice versa. Thus, we
might rephrase the question: What is
not skin?

In the beginning, it is a question of
skin. Not yet a question of bones but
of skin—dermal layers that hide
nothing… nothing but other dermal
layers. Humpty Dumpty need not
have fallen to be faulted, for every fer-
tilized egg is always already divided
between vegetal and animal poles. The
process of embryonic development
involves cellular division and further
differentiation. Through a quasi-
cybernetic process governed by preprogrammed DNA, the pluripotentiality
of the ovum is limited in ways that
allow for the articulation of different
organic structures and functions. Cells
multiply by division to create a hollow
ball called a blastomere.

This sphere eventually invaginates to form a lined pocket comprised of two layers known as the endoderm and the ectoderm, which, in turn, partially peel away to generate a third surface known as the mesoderm. The mature organism develops from these three dermal layers. Since the organism as a whole is formed by a complex of dermal layers, the body is, in effect, nothing but layers of skin in which interiority and exteriority are thoroughly convoluted.

The phrase "light construction," so ably defined and explored by Terry Riley, reflects such dermal convolution. The result is a transfiguring of the very architecture of skin and surface. Surface, for the architects whose work is included in this exhibition, is no longer what it was for classical modernists. In his catalogue essay, Riley writes: "That all of the preceding projects might be referred to as 'transparent' suggests a newfound interest in a term long associated with the architecture of the modern movement. Yet the tension between viewer and object implied by the use of the architectural facade as a veiling membrane indicates a departure from past attitudes and a need to reexamine the word *transparency* as it relates to architecture"(p. 11). Riley develops his reexamination of transparency by contrasting it with translucence through a series of binary oppositions such as clarity/ambiguity or penetration/delay. Drawing on Jean Starobinski's interpretation of the gaze, Riley concludes that a new, very unmodern surface emerges: "the facade becomes an interposed veil, triggering a subjective relationship by distancing the viewer of the building from the space or forms within and isolating the viewer within from the outside world." (p. 10)

View of audience at the symposium.

As a way of advancing debate, I would like to make three observations about Riley's analysis. First, there is a closer relationship between transparency and translucence than Riley suggests. Though not immediately evident, it is precisely transparency that leads to translucence. It is important to realize that the polarity of surface and depth is isomorphic with the polarity of interiority and exteriority. When depth becomes transparent, it is another surface; and when interiority becomes transparent, it is exteriorized. As everything becomes transparent, depth and interiority vanish. Paradoxically, the result of such radical transparency is not lucidity but translucence. In a certain sense, depth and interiority—even when they remain hidden—secure or ground surface as well as exteriority. If depth is surface and inferiority is exteriority, then the very proliferation of surface renders it not only opaque but enigmatic. This enigma is what renders surface profound.

Second, the profundity of surface and superficiality of profundity make it necessary to rethink both surface and depth. When depth and interiority disappear, surface is transformed. Surface, in other words, no longer can be conceived as it was when it was the opposite of depth and inferiority; it becomes something different, something other. Riley offers a gesture toward this insight when he introduces the notion of the veil and, by extension, emphasizes the *between*—or, I would prefer, the liminal character of surface. But no sooner does he offer this notion than he reinscribes it within precisely the opposites it undoes. The veil, we are told, distances the viewer from the space or forms within and isolates the viewer within the outside world. If, however, it's surface all the way down, then does the membrane any longer separate in this way? I would suggest that we must rethink surface as interface, or, more precisely, interfacing.

Third, interfaces must be read in terms of information processes. With this observation, I return to the question of skin with which I began. Though we usually think of skin as the sack that envelops the body's organs, it is actually the largest organ of the body. This organ is not only the interface where body meets world but, like the organs that develop from it, is the interface of the so-called material and the so-called immaterial. This interface, as noted, is a quasi-cybernetic process governed by preprogrammed DNA. The skin, in other words, is an information process in which material realities appear to be immaterial processes. If, however, the entire organism develops from dermal layers, then all of the organs—even the skeleton itself—are transparent information processes. Information processes are not merely displayed on the screen of the skin but pervade the very depths of the organism. In this play of data, surface and depth, as well

as exteriority and inferiority, are reinscribed. Riley is right when he argues that veils veil other veils. But, I believe, he is wrong when he insists that veils separate rather than interface.

To summarize: transparency that becomes translucent; surfaces that become interfaces; interfaces that are informational processes. Herein lies the depth of skin.

Mark Taylor teaches humanities at Williams College in Williamstown, Massachusetts. His books include *Disfiguring: Art, Architecture, Religion* (Chicago: University of Chicago Press, 1992), *Nots* (Chicago: University of Chicago Press, 1993) and *Imagologies: Media Philosophy* (New York and London: Routledge, 1994).

LIGHT CONSTRUCTION
SYMPOSIUM
HUGH DUTTON

Hugh Dutton

There are two kinds of lightness in light architecture. First, lightweight construction, and second, light itself. In light architecture, both are important. We can define a building as structure, which supports it, and skin, which keeps the weather out. Lightweight structures allow the skin, through transparency or luminous surfaces, to respond to light itself. As regards structure, technological advances in the building industry and developments in structural engineering have removed structure from walls and surfaces. High-performance materials, such as reinforced concrete, steel and, more recently, composites have allowed a concentration of structure. Developments in structural engineering skills have further contributed to "lightweightness," with a greater understanding of how buildings behave, as has the recent use of computers in analyzing complex, interactive and statically indeterminate structures like the dome of the Seis de Jeneval in Paris, which the engineering firm of Peter Rice, Martin Francis and Ian Ritchie (RFR) has just completed.

One project in the development of non-linear analysis that allows large tensile structures to be understood is Richard Rogers's Channel Four Headquarters in London, in which the glass is stabilized by purely tensile cable nets. The cable net is curved in two directions, with each direction of the cable's tension against the other. In regard to skin, the gradual removing of structure has allowed the skin to become more ephemeral— first transparent, then translucent— because it no longer has to hold up the building. This allows light itself to play a larger part in the architectural composition.

Glaiman, Epstein and Vidal: Arc Union offices, 50 Avenue Montaigne, Paris, 1994. Consulting engineers: RFR, Paris (Peter Rice, Hugh Dutton, Nicolas Prouvé, William Matthews). (Photo ©A.M.)

Pei Cobb Freed & Partners: Pyramid Inversée, the Louvre, Paris, 1994. Consulting engineers: RFR, Paris (Peter Rice, Henry Bardsley, Lionel Penisson). (Photo ©RFR)

Recent developments in curtain wall technology have created new possibilities, not only in glass, but also in architectural fabrics. Fritting is a process of baking paint onto glass in which the paint actually becomes part of the glass surface. One can also manufacture glass with a translucent film that has been sandwiched between two sheets of glass and a laminate. A special treatment for glass also allows it to be used on a floor, so one can actually walk on a translucent floor. Printed glass technology has been around for a long time but is now much improved with technology. There is also the possibility of laminating stone; recent technology has permitted the lamination of very thin stone, down to about one millimeter thick, onto glass. And, there is another quite simple technique of putting a perforated

steel mesh between two sheets of glass and a laminate. This process permits a reflectivity on the outside of the metal. From the inside, because of the relative light values, it is still very transparent.

Examples of projects affected by different technologies being developed in Japan include liquid crystal glass, which, when an electronic current is passed through it, changes from a transparent to a translucent state. In its translucent state, it can be used as a source of image projection. There is also thermochrome glass, which, when the glass is heated, becomes opaque and translucent.

In insulated glass, different treatments allow reflectivity and limit heat absorption while affecting the quality of the light that comes through the

Cité des Sciences et de L'Industrie. View of curtain wall.

Adrien Fainsilber: Musee national des sciences, des techniques et des industries, La Cité des Sciences et de l'Industrie, Parc de la Villette, Paris, 1985. Consulting engineers for the "glass boxes" on the main facade: RFR, Paris (Peter Rice, Martin Francis, Ian Ritchie, Henry Bardsley, Gilles Besançon, Guy Deshayes, Hugh Dutton, Jean-Paul Etienne, Jane Wernick). (Photo ©RFR)

Odile Decq and Benoit Cornette: Banque Populaire de l'Ouest et d'Armorique, Rennes, France, 1989. Consulting engineers for the facade: RFR, Paris (Peter Rice, Guy Deshayes, Hugh Dutton, Alistair Lenczner, Lionel Penisson). (Photo ©ArchiPress)

Odile Decq and Benoit Cornette: Banque Populaire de l'Ouest et d'Armorique, Rennes, France, 1989. Consulting engineers for the facade: RFR, Paris (Peter Rice, Guy Deshayes, Hugh Dutton, Alistair Lenczner, Lionel Penisson). (Photo ©RFR)

glass. Most of this technology was developed at RFR with Peter Rice. With the facade of the Banque Populaire de l'Ouest et d'Armorique (1989) in Rennes, HDA actually pulled the wind-bracing structure two meters away from the glass. The little sticks are actually the only connection between the glass surface and the structure. So the structure is completely outside, and the glass surface is on the inside.

HDA just finished a project in Paris that exploits the structural capacity of transparent glass, allowing us to create a transparent corner, and a transparent roof. In the Pyramide Inversée (inverted pyramid) for the Louvre (1991), designed by I. M. Pei, the reflective nature of the glass is exploited to its full potential. This entails a mixture of architectural fabric and glass fiber with a Teflon coating on it, which has a translucent quality; mixed with glass, it produces a luminous, translucent surface. A project that we did with Peter Rice at La Villette, the Cité des Sciences et de l'Industrie by Adrian Fainsibler, is one of the first projects to really exploit what I think is important in the use of glass surface—its own structural capacity. In this case, all of the glass is suspended; each piece hangs from the one above it. The key detail is a ball bearing, which guarantees that there is no bending or twisting effect on the glass. The glass is loaded purely along its axis, where it is strongest.

I would like to close with an example of a project we finished in Paris, an office development at 50 Avenue Montaigne, which I think takes lightness to an extreme. This applies not only to the supporting structure,

Patrick Berger, Jean Paul Viguier and Jean-Francois Jodry: greenhouses for Parc Andre Citroen-Cevennes, Paris,1966. Landscape architects: Alain Provost and Gilles Clement. Structural engineers: RFR, Paris (Peter Rice, Hugh Dutton, Henry Bardsley, B. V., M. D., Guy Deshayes, Nicolas Prouvé, P. C.). (Photo ©RFR)

which in this case is a fan of cables pulled back to the concrete structure, but also to the structural capacity of the glass itself (we have quite big pieces of toughened glass, spanning up to 3.80 meters). The glass is fritted, which creates a diffuse light source at nighttime and disperses the view through it during the day. The glass is suspended 24 meters high (each piece suspended from the one above it) and is 60 meters wide.

Greenhouse facade detail.

LIGHT
CONSTRUCTION
SYMPOSIUM
EEVA-LIISA PELKONEN

Just after I received the invitation to attend this symposium, I saw a documentary on Finnish television called "Jean Nouvel—The Man in Black." In presenting his work, Nouvel clarified his approach to making architecture. His remarks are helpful in locating the tendency in contemporary architecture toward "light constructions" on the map of the intellectual and artistic culture of the postwar era.

Most important, Nouvel emphasized the need for a particular problem-solving attitude in each design task, as opposed to the application of preexisting formal solutions; only then can architecture have any social significance. He also discussed the need for realization; that is, architecture cannot exist as a mere idea but must engage a particular social, economic and political situation as well as a site condition. His final comment was perhaps the most telling—that he can never stop thinking about the future.

Helmut Richter: Brunnerstraße Housing, Vienna, 1991.

In contemporary European architecture Nouvel is not alone in believing that architecture can and should become engaged in the society at large. This belief is the main premise of the twentieth-century avant-garde: art and architecture are integrally linked to the social and the political and can therefore enhance transformation and change.

Like his predecessors within the avant-garde tradition, Nouvel actively participates in the intellectual culture of his time. It comes as no surprise that, nourished by the rarefied milieu in France from the 1960s onward, Nouvel is disposed toward Existential Marxism, particularly the ideas of Henri Lefebvre. Nouvel's belief that architecture should result from working with a complex set of factors related to a particular architectural task, that is, of a certain critique, recalls Lefebvre's *Critique de la vie quotidienne* (*Critique of Everyday Life*).

The book illustrates the main premise of Existential Marxism as a social theory suited to comprehending the conditions and contradictions of advanced industrial society. Nouvel's notion of the particular also comes close to Lefebvre, who emphasized the concrete and the everyday—the analysis of the human situation. What is important is that critique is not simply a *knowledge* of everyday life, but a knowledge of the means to transform it. Therefore, just as Existential Marxism can be essentially understood as a "philosophy of action," Nouvel's approach to architecture might likewise be called an "architecture of action." As Nouvel's comment about the future reveals, like Lefebvre, he remains an eternal optimist anticipating utopian possibilities.

Volker Giencke: Botanical Garden, Graz, 1995.

Botanical Garden. interior view

What interests me in the context of our theme is how the material condition of "light construction" corresponds to such an approach to making architecture. The obsession with glass in contemporary architecture helps us understand this correlation between "lightness" and a certain "tone" behind the work. We should remember that the typical building types that have been made with glass architecture—the glass house, the railway station, the exhibition hall and the commercial arcade—are all sites for the ultimate modern experience: urban drifting, a moment in which we willingly surrender ourselves to the sensuous stimulus of the crowds. As the theorist Susan Buck-Morss has pointed out, these building types were meant for "transient purposes" and to be experienced by the masses rather than to be used for individual contemplation. Important for our discussion is that since glass architecture has

always been "engineered" architecture, the following historical analogy exists: materiality and structure took formal strategies just as the mass experience took over mere contemplation. I would argue that it is exactly this correspondence between "tectonics" and "experience" in the Benjaminian sense that makes contemporary architecture so interesting. Therefore, I would like to oppose "lightness" as a material condition to the formal (classical) approach to architecture. Lightness emphasizes temporality rather than a static notion of space; active engagement rather than passive contemplation.

Such a move away from formal strategies toward the emphasis of materiality and structure has parallels in postwar art: the tendency of the European avant-garde has been to reject the kind of abstraction inherent in the classical heritage of modernism. According to the Danish painter Asger Jorn, the new "materialist art" aimed to engage the

Botanical Garden. Exterior view

particular human condition rather than be a mere object of contemplation. Jorn, who was a member of CoBrA and later the Situationist International, an international avant-garde group strongly influenced by Lefebvre, held that European art was corrupted by its classical heritage, its metaphysical overvaluation of reason and the idea. The new materialist attitude toward art and life must involve the expression of natural rhythms and passions, rather than seek to subordinate activity to a sovereign meaning.

Similarly, by means of a heightened sensibility toward materiality and structure, contemporary architecture, particularly in continental Europe—Nouvel provides a good example—enhances engagement by fighting the hegemony of form and meaning in Western architectural tradition—hence lightness. Through "lightness," and "light constructions," contemporary architecture has discovered its potential to convey a character and

ambience that makes architecture resistant both to the metaphysical abyss as well as to the pessimistic traits of postwar thought. What I mean by character and ambience is a certain tone and ethos of the work. More subtle and elusive than meaning can ever be, ethos tells us about the disposition of the author without making any final judgments. Similarly, on a material level, lightness can be opposed to the formal approach to architecture: while form and meaning aim to fix things, "lightness," as I understand it, is about letting things loose, which manifests the utopian impulse within the work.

Eeva-Liisa Pelkonen (M.Arch Tampere University of Technology, 1990; M.E.D. Yale School of Architecture, 1994) teaches architectural design and theory at Yale School of Architecture. She is the author of *Achtung Architektur! Image and Phantasm in Contemporary Austrian Architecture* (Cambridge and Chicago: MIT Press and Graham Foundation, 1996). She is a recipient of Fulbright Scholarship and Graham Foundation Grant for Advanced Studies in the Fine Arts. In 1992-1992 she was a research fellow of the Austrian Ministry of Science and Research. She is currently a fellow of the Finnish Academy and enrolled in the Ph.D. program for architectural history and theory at Columbia University. Ms. Pelkonen is a partner of Brooks + Pelkonen architects.

LIGHT CONSTRUCTION
SYMPOSIUM
GUY NORDENSON

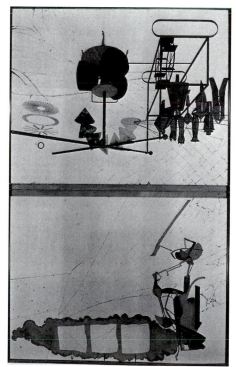

Marcel Duchamp: *The Bride Stripped Bare by Her Bachelors, Even,* 1915–23.

In the early 1970s America was introduced to deconstruction via the works of, among others, Paul de Man and Harold Bloom—in particular, their books *Blindness and Insight and Anxiety of Influence,* respectively, through which many people were first exposed to the ideas of Jacques Derrida. This was the period during which Peter Eisenman's Institute for Architecture and Urban Studies was active, when Rem Koolhaas published his *Delirious New York* and when the Vietnam War came to an end. I mention all this here to propose that we consider that the work which Terence Riley has put together in this exhibition has developed from seeds sown around that time. I believe that this is a body of work that closely reflects the ideas current at the time, and those of Derrida in particular. In his essay "Structure, Sign and Play," presented at Johns Hopkins University in 1966, Derrida reviewed Levi-Strauss's

Buckminster Fuller: *Project for a Geodesic Dome over Midtown Manhattan*, 1962.

works in detail and questioned the structuralist idea that totalization is impossible because the field of inquiry is too vast, rather than, as Derrida argued, because while the field is finite it is elusive because of a lack of determined origin and its nature of constant play. Here Derrida aligns himself with the critique of the Enlightenment—from Isaiah Berlin to Werner Heisenberg. If the Enlightenment was inspired by Newton's successes, our own era, not surprisingly, has undergone a sea of change as the consequences of the new sciences of relativity, quantum electrodynamics and particle physics work their influence through the culture.

This brings us back to the subject of light and construction, or light and

Spider's web.

matter. There is a wonderful book by the late physicist Richard Feynman called *QED: The Strange Theory of Light and Matter.* In a footnote Feynman points out that Heisenberg's principle of uncertainty is a vestige of determinism. If we accept the probabilistic nature of matter and light's interaction, then there is no problem of uncertainty. Rather, events are the product of probability amplitudes.

This is a difficult thing to accept and convey. Italo Calvino describes this world as one "of minute particles of humors and sensations, a fine dust of atoms like everything else that goes to make up the ultimate substance of the multiplicity of things."

I would like to offer a few concepts about light that, from my perspective, are relevant to the exhibition. First I propose that as "light" refers to the light of our sun, we are particularly interested in the strange facts of the interaction of light and matter. The light inside a building is radiated by the "matter" of construction. Light on glass sets off an interaction (scattering) and the glass emits a spectrum of light-energy. Light and matter or light and structure are always interacting, absorbing, emitting and intermingling. Second, there is the lightness of bits, the universe of digital representation and the pattern of chaos revealed in the new telescope of the computer. This relates, of course, to chance, to Marcel Duchamp and John Cage and back to quantum physics. But most of all, it reveals the mysterious beauty and order of turbulence and upheaval. Third, there is that lightness championed by

Buckminster Fuller. Fuller, our twentieth-century Emerson, promised in 1969 that "the ever acceleratingly dangerous impasse of world-opposed politicians and ideological dogmas would be resolved by the computer." He identified and promoted that digital ephemeralization. For him, the lightest touch was best, as in Jean Prouvé's Tropical House and his own Dymaxion House. It is the lightness of nomads at home on Spaceship Earth. Fourth, and related to Fuller's ideas, there is a lightness of frugality. It is interesting to note that the visual imagery in many of the projects recalls the space and light of television and film.

If we consider the critic John Berger's description of perspectival space as a safe and transpose it to television and computer media, we can perhaps better recognize the continuity that exists in the business of capturing and preserving wealth. Facades are still in the art and business of containing and projecting economic value. Perhaps instead, as in a Bedouin tent or Prouvé's Tropical House, our interest could extend not to the representation of wealth but to the preservation of commonwealth through building lightness and frugality. Fifth, and finally, there is the lightness of being. Think of Duchamp, Cage, Milan Kundera and countless others.

In closing, I would like to recount a little Zen story called "No Water, No

Time magazine cover, 1968.

Moon." When the nun Chiyono studied Zen under Bukko Engaku, she was unable to attain the fruits of meditation for a long time. At last, one moonlit night, she was carrying water in an old pail bound with bamboo. The bamboo broke and the bottom fell out of the pail. At that moment, Chiyono was set free. In commemoration, she wrote a poem:

*In this way and that I tried to save
the old pail
since the bamboo strip was
weakening and about to break,
until at last, the bottom fell out.
No more water in the pail.
No more moon in the water !*

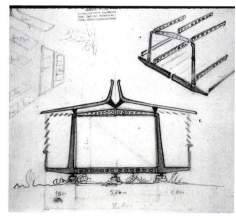

Jean Prouve: Tropical House sketch. 1950.

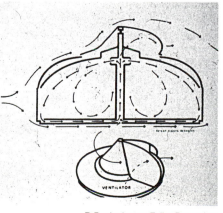

R Buckminster: Fuller Dymaxion
air circulation diagram. 1946

Guy Nordenson has a structural
engineering practice in New York and
is associate professor of architecture
at Princeton University. His design
for the 480 meter cable stayed Rio
Grande de Loiza Bridge in Carolinas
Puerto Rico is scheduled to be
completed in 1999 and he is
consulting on the design of Richard
Meier's Chiesa di Anno 2000 in Rome.
He is editing a collection of 100
essays on Buckminster Fuller for
publication next year.

LIGHT CONSTRUCTION
SYMPOSIUM
K. MICHAEL HAYS

I would like to push the discussion out a little bit, as I think Eeva Pelkonen and Guy Nordenson have already begun to do, and think more about the larger cultural and historical context of some of the work in this exhibition. Terence Riley himself begins his catalogue essay with a kind of comparison between current interests in the psychological implications of diverse glazing surfaces and Ludwig Hilberseimer's perception of modernity's rationalist uses of glass. What Riley does not mention is that Hilberseimer's kind of modernism also had a psychological correlate. Siegfried Kracauer writes about the psychological correlate of modern architecture, the logic of the repetition and transparency of modern architecture. In his essay "The Mass Ornament," he uses the Tiller Girls, an American dance troupe similar to the Rockettes that performed in Berlin in the twenties, as a kind of mock psychological paradigm for what could be thought of as Hilberseimer's architecture: "When they formed an undulating snake, they radiantly illustrated the virtues of a conveyor belt. When they tapped their feet in fast tempo, it sounded like 'business … business.' When they kicked their legs high with mathematical precision, they joyously affirmed the progress of rationalization. And when they kept repeating the same movements without ever interrupting their routine, one envisioned an uninterrupted chain of autos gliding from the factories into the world."[1]

I am trying to get at a kind of model of the logic of the series. On the other side of this kind of ecstatic psychological model is Georg Lukács's reminder of the relentless and unfruitful repetitive labor of the proletariat. Modernism had a depth model—Hilberseimer's model—of psychological experience that was a correlate of the formal research. When Riley talks about the shift from the logic of repetitive series, or the formal logic, to a logic of surface, what is the corresponding psychological model and where does it come from? Let's call it "depthlessness" or "lightness." Where does that mode of perception come from? Eeva Pelkonen has already suggested the sixties; Nordenson, the seventies. I'll go back one more decade and suggest that this model actually had its roots in the urban developments of the fifties when, for example, electronic advertising was used in American commercial

Girls at a Rehearsal, from The Mass Ornament.

Siegfried Kracauer: The Mass Ornament, 1929.

cities on a scale previously unknown. Large-scale color printing on billboards, as we know from people like Peter Blake and Robert Venturi, began to be the primary surfaces seen. It was also at this time that television became available to a large number of people. The decentralization of the distribution of goods from urban centers out into the suburbs fundamentally began to change the mode of perception from a depth model—a spatial model, a formal model—to the logic of the perception of surfaces. What we are seeing may need to be tied historically to a development that was well underway in America in the fifties.

Jean Baudrillard captures something when he suggests that instead of the logic of the series, our psychological investment is now in a non-reflecting surface, an immanent surface on which operations unfold, the smooth operational surface of communication. Baudrillard further says that with the television image—television being the ultimate and perfect object for this new era—our own body and the whole surrounding universe become a controlled screen. My point is to suggest that popular culture—a kind of absent, or partially absent cause—and some of the projects in the exhibition, or their "sensibility," as Terence Riley describes it, are also symptoms of shifts and developments in the mode of perception given by popular culture. It's not an

Left: Greg Lynn;
right: K. Michael Hays.

indictment of the work to say that it collapses into popular culture. Rather, I think we see now what is becoming a kind of salvage operation that is trying to redeem most perceptions in popular culture—media, music, video, television—in new kinds of surfaces.

This is important because some of the fundamental critical models, like Marxism or even deconstruction, will therefore have to be revised. Those that engage popular culture, such as Marxism, critical theory and deconstruction, have been primarily negational models. We have two specific and powerful models. One is Kenneth Frampton's notion that architecture has an inertia or a resistance to popular culture. This model will necessarily be modulated by some of the works in the exhibition to allow for their redemptive stance toward popular culture. The other model, Bernard Tschumi's

poststructuralist "De-, Dis-, Ex," will have to be modified to acknowledge reappropriation, reconstruction, redemption and this kind of salvaging operation, which is a much more affirmative stance, relative to popular culture.

NOTE
1. Siegfried Kracauer, "The Mass Ornament," in *The Mass Ornament: Weimar Essays*, trans. and ed. Thomas Y. Levin (Cambridge, Mass. and London: Harvard University Press, 1995), 69–70.

K. Michael Hays is Professor of Architectural Theory and Director of the Ph.D. program at the Graduate School of Design, Harvard University. He is founder and editor of *Assemblage*. Hays received a Doctor of Philosophy degree in History, Theory and Criticism from the Massachusetts Institute of Technology. His published work focuses on ideological issues in the history of the avant-garde and on current debates in architecture and critical theory. His book, *Modern Architecture and the Posthumanist Subject* was published in 1992 by MIT Press. *Unprecedented Realism: The Architecture of Machado and Silvetti* was published in 1995 by Princeton Architectural Press. He is currently working on an anthology of architecture theory since 1968, to be published in collaboration with the Graduate School of Architecture, Planning and Preservation Columbia University.

LIGHT CONSTRUCTION
SYMPOSIUM
GREG LYNN

The exhibition allows multiple threads to be pulled through the work because as Terence Riley has said, there are enough issues without condensing things into a style or movement, to allow for multiple readings. Some of the organizational and formal research in the projects might constitute a kind of "light underground," meaning that a building can be conceived and conceptualized as light without necessarily being lightweight. This can be seen as a *concept* of lightness, as opposed to a *phenomenon* of lightness, which moves toward transparency and dematerialization. As an initial provocation, one of the most overrated and undercriticized concepts in architecture is the persistent myth that buildings must stand up. A number of projects in the exhibition, "Light Construction" do

Bernard Tschumi: Glass Video Gallery, Groningen, the Netherlands, 1990

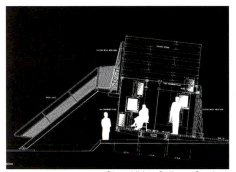

Glass Video Gallery. Section.

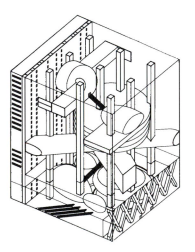

Rem Koolhaas–O.M.A.: Bibliothèque Nationale de France, Paris, 1989.

not stand up but explore alternative concepts of structure—such as leaning, hanging and suspension—that are fundamental formal principles related to the concept of lightness, and do not look to gravity as a single force emanating from the earth. There is a kind of subterfuge in saying that transparency is the only interpretation of lightness and that lightweight and light are identical. It is necessary at this point to back up from the experiential questions of what would make a building *light* and reconsider concepts on which we could found or ground light architecture, instead of formulating a light architecture as a resistance to gravity, which is what our discipline has been founded on. Lightness suggests that we might suspend strategies based on notions of simple gravity and look toward multiple gravities.

Toyo Ito: Sendai Mediatheque, Japan, 1995.

Three projects in the exhibition propose complex responses to multiple gravities, Rem Koolhaas's Bibliothèque Nationale de France in Paris (1989), in the catalogue text is described as a floating object held behind a transparent screen. But before that tectonic articulation was ever developed, there had to be a concept of an over-structuring, in an almost Corbusian manner, of the building so that these volumes could be suspended conceptually in the space. Likewise, in Bernard Tschumi's Glass Video Gallery in Groningen, the Netherlands (1990), a very lightweight structure is developed, but the ground on which that structure is supported is sloped. Finally, in Toyo Ito's Sendai Mediatheque in Japan (1995), the columns, instead of being seen as solid structural elements, are conceived as towers of latticework in the center. These are all new concepts of structure and support,

what I consider light concepts. I do not want to oppose the *conceptual* light to the *phenomenal* light because in each one of these projects, I think there is a very strong sense of invention as to what lightweight materials can do.

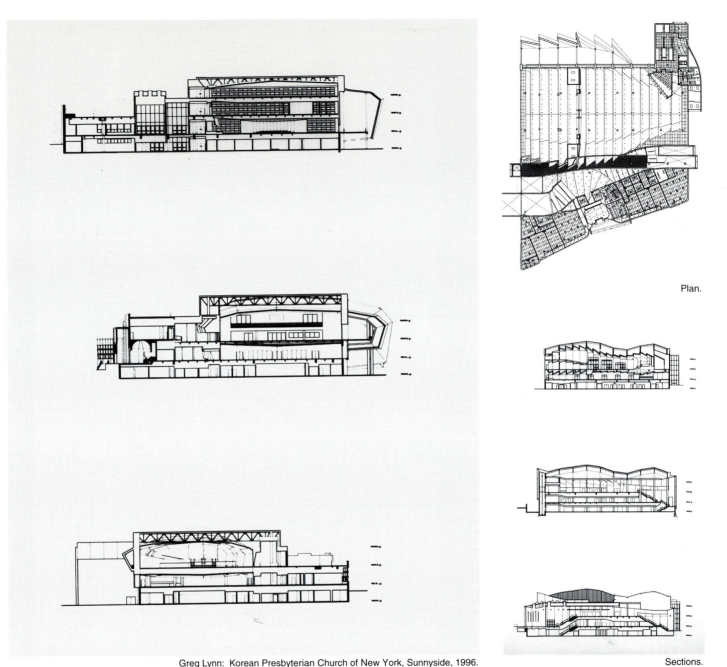

Plan.

Sections.

Greg Lynn: Korean Presbyterian Church of New York, Sunnyside, 1996.
Sections.

**Greg Lynn is adjunct assistant
professor of architecture at Columbia
University and principal of the
architectural design firm FORM**

LIGHT CONSTRUCTION SYMPOSIUM
TOYO ITO

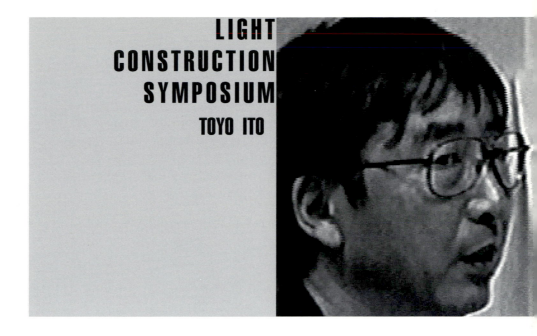

At one time the architect's main project was to create an architecture and an urban space that fluidly utilized and integrated the local topography and natural forces such as wind, water and light. But during the modern period, architecture's relationship with nature ended and the urban as architectural space became a rigidly "geometric," artificial space. Today, however, through the penetration of various new forms of media, fluidity is regaining validity. As more urban and architectural space is controlled by the media, it is becoming increasingly cinematic and fluid. It has become a transparent kind of space. Therefore, I think we are now forced to admit more openness and flexibility to this closed and artificial urban and architectural space, combining the fluidity created by the media with the fluidity of nature.

This fluidity was the major focus of our installation in London. Two of the structural components we used were liquid crystal and glass. For me, these materials refer metaphorically to similar things in our physical bodies. On the one hand, our material bodies are a primitive mechanism, taking in air and water and circulating them. On the other hand, there is another kind of body that consists of circulating electronic information—the body that is connected to the rest of the world through various forms of media, including computer microchips. Today, we are being forced to think about how to architecturally combine these two different bodies and how to find an appropriate space for the emerging third body. This is why I have been completely focused on the idea of lightness in architecture.

In the Tower of the Winds, there were two major concerns. One had to do with the skin of the structure, which is made with perforated aluminum panels. It represents the constantly

Toyo Ito: Shimosuwa Municipal Museum, Shimosuwa, Japan, 1993.

Shimosuwa Municipal Museum. view of exterior

Toyo Ito: Tower of the Winds
Yokohama, Japan, 1986 (dismantled 1995)

changing quality of skin over time. The other concern was the visualization of daily urban phenomena, such as traffic, noise, or wind.

We also built a small museum on a lakeside. Although the building itself has a specific formal configuration, our main concern was how to present the building as a reflection of other phenomenal conditions such as fog or rainbows on the surface of the water. We conceived the aluminum surface as a reflective device operating between the town and its natural surroundings. The exterior, a linen-like skin, is produced and manipulated with the aid of a computer.

Although not exhibited in "Light Construction," our Mediatheque project, located in Sendai, north of Tokyo, is effective in illustrating my theories. The program combines an

Toyo Ito: Sendai Mediatheque, Japan, 1995

art gallery and a library. The building consists of seven horizontal slabs supported by twelve structural tubes. The structure is made of meshed steel. The inside of the tubes can be utilized as a transportation system, for other mechanical services such as plumbing and electricity or for circulating information. The larger tubes, which look like three stems, are open as void spaces. The natural light from above flows into those vertical voids. The tubes do not formally connote a tree; rather, the interior space evokes the inside of a tree, in terms of the circulation of water and other activities. The tubes are covered by translucent glass. The lighting devices are placed discreetly underneath the bottom of the tubes and when lit, the tubes become illuminated from the inside out. The exterior skin is composed of glass, which is reflective at the top, becoming gradually more transparent toward the bottom. During the day, the glass reflects the outside on its surface; at night, it reveals what is going on inside.

Toyo Ito graduated from Tokyo University's Department of Architecture in 1965 and is currently principal of Toyo Ito and Associates, Architects. He has lectured extensively throughout Japan, Europe and the United States, and his work has appeared in numerous exhibitions internationally. Ito's firm received the Togo Murano Award for the design of the guest house for Sapporo Breweries in Hokkaido, Japan in 1990. Recent projects include the I-Building in Asakusabashi and the Yatsushiro Fire Station, both in Japan.

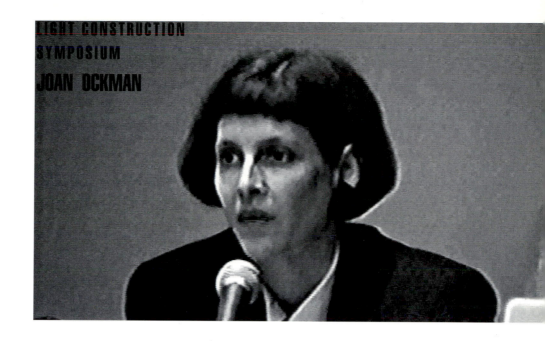

I'd like to begin by commenting on Herbert Muschamp's review of this provocative exhibition that appeared in the *New York Times* this morning. Like Muschamp, we all naturally will wish to quibble one way or another with Terence Riley's inclusions and exclusions, and I would agree that less might have been more in this instance. However, I want to take issue with the review's main thrust. Muschamp suggested that the exhibition is ultimately about taste. Now while, historically speaking, MoMA has a long record of architectural taste-making, I do not necessarily believe that taste is the primary issue here. And that is why I wish a few of the projects in the exhibition had not been included. If a more succinct articulation of the show's thesis had been provided, critics would not be able to suggest that "Light Construction" is a matter of taste-making.

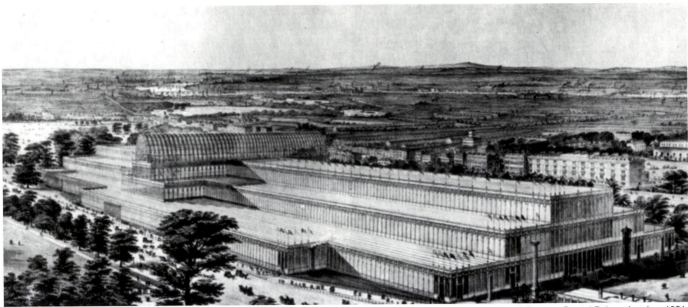

Joseph Paxton: Crystal Palace, London, 1851.

But if the exhibition does not merely reflect a current taste for the sophisticated use of glass and a penchant for lightweight building technology, then what is it about? Terence Riley speaks of an "emerging sensibility" in his introduction. It's not clear to me what a sensibility is in this context, let alone an emerging one. Maybe "tendency" or "style" would have been a better characterization. But the main reason I don't believe that "Light Construction" can be dismissed as a matter of taste is that these buildings lay claim to being connected, at least potentially, to a new mode of production—a new mode of construction and a new relationship between architecture and the city. As Walter Benjamin writes in his essay "Paris, Capital of the Nineteenth Century," "Construction fills the role of the unconscious." In this vein Benjamin interpreted the arcade as a crystallization of nineteenth-century culture, a building type key to the advent of modernity. Are the buildings in the current exhibition comparable today with respect to postmodernity? Can an architecture of "light construction" be said to be—for example—a materialization of the advancing forces of dematerialization in our culture?

I found Hugh Dutton's presentation quite suggestive. I'm not a technical expert, so it raised many questions for me. I'm eager to know how extraordinary, how extravagant all these new ways of treating glass are. To paraphrase Buckminster Fuller, how much do these new glass surfaces weigh? Are they *really* light? Are they environmentally "correct"? Are these technologies at all likely to become normative; do they have the potential to supersede current building practice? Bernard Tschumi mentioned the construction industry's resistance to accepting new ways of building. Are the new treatments of glass we are seeing strictly haute couture, or will they trickle down to the mainstream of building construction? It is worth recalling that the development of architectural glass—going back several hundred years—was directed up until about the first quarter of this century toward transparency, toward the perfection of an ever larger plate of glass to a point of perfect clarity. But now that transparency as a see-through characteristic has been technologically mastered, it's hardly surprising to find that it is no longer the issue. The mastery of the transparent glass plane makes way for more complex and interesting uses of this marvelous material.

Historically speaking, we can discern two seemingly antithetical points of inception for the glass or transparent dream with respect to modern architecture culture. Certainly the Crystal Palace, designed by Joseph Paxton and erected in 1851, is one such point. It constitutes the canonical beginning of modern architecture in Sigfried Giedion's *Space, Time and Architecture* as well as in most other classic modernist historiographies. In its day the Crystal Palace was not just a building but an event. Its reception was sensational. People made pilgrimages from all over Europe to see this large glass building derived from the typology of the greenhouse conjoined with the railway shed and built for the first great international trade fair. A very common perception was a sense of dematerialization, of dissolution. The

Crystal Palace. View of interior.

interior of the building was painted mostly blue, a color that blended into the blue of the sky. In its vastness the building seemed to "melt into air," to evoke Marx's famous words, to become a kind of dream landscape. A contemporary called it "a spectacle, incomparable and fairylike." It inaugurated a new optics.

Symbolically, the Crystal Palace stood for a world that was progress-oriented, scientific and practical. Constructed in record time from economical, modular and demountable parts, it was the epitome of rational engineering. At the same time, however, like the contemporary arcade buildings, it housed the proliferating products of a nascent consumer capitalism. The clarities and lucidities of structure were dissolved not only by the

building's new optical scale, but also by its phantasmagoria of endless goods. Rationalism yielded to spectacle and surreality.

Now let's jump a hundred years, to 1958 to be precise. Peter and Alison Smithson had just returned from a first trip to the United States having witnessed the array of new curtain wall buildings springing up on Park Avenue (the first of them, Lever House, had been completed six years earlier, in fact precisely on the centenary of the Crystal Palace). The Smithsons made the following observation: "Glass and metal-faced buildings give the maximum light reflection into the street. And this in itself is a contribution to the city. And there are, moreover, magical distortions when two straight up and down buildings are opposite one another. A blue glass city, no matter

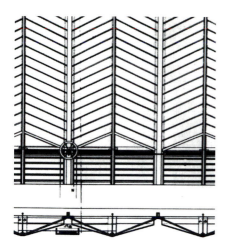

Crystal Palace. Detail plan and elevation
of the transept roofing.

how organizationally banal, is never optically boring."

What had changed in the course of a century? One may say that Park Avenue represents the transformation of the Crystal Palace into a normative urban phenomenon: the glass building as a metonymic emblem of the modernist city rather than as a singular spectacle in a park. The postwar International Style turned the Crystal Palace inside out, so to speak, and multiplied it. And now, another half century later, we may ask the same question with respect to the glass buildings of our own day. What has changed? What distinguishes the most exciting buildings in "Light Construction"—buildings like Toyo Ito's Tower of Winds, Jean Nouvel's Cartier Foundation and Jacques Herzog and Pierre de Meuron's Goetz Collection—from their progenitors? Certainly one of the things that the exhibition reveals is that we are still bedazzled, thrilled, hypnotized by the paradoxical optics of glass, by reflective and transparent and translucent and changeable luminous surfaces. But what innovation has postmodernity contributed to this tradition? Is it just refinement, or are there new constructional principles—technical and cultural—operative in these contemporary buildings?

There is a second glass paradigm to be found at the origins of modernity, and this one brings us closer to the more metaphysical connotations of the word "light" on which Terence Riley plays in his exhibition title. If the Crystal Palace was a profane and secular dream, then the Crystal Cathedral—the one, for example, in Lyonel Feininger's woodcut accompanying the founding proclamation of the Bauhaus, or in the imagery of Mies's two early glass skyscrapers—represents a new religion of modern architecture. The Crystal Cathedral is a vehicle of visionary and utopian thought, and as such a privileged icon of the early modern avant-garde. Unlike the Enlightenment tradition of glass, that of the Crystal Cathedral has to do with the spiritual mission of architecture as art, with introverted as much as extroverted experience. It harks back to the "lightness" of Gothic architecture, to stained glass and highly attenuated structure. In this tradition glass tends to be

associated with crystalline substances and jewellike stones, with the alchemical transformation of base materials into precious ones— the basic recipe for glass, remember, is little more than sand plus lime plus heat. It thereby embodies mystical and transcendental meanings. We should recall that Paul Scheerbart's book *Glass Architecture* and the apocalyptic projects of Bruno Taut's Glass Chain call for colored light and magical effects, not for transparency and lucidity.

Actually, Scheerbart's idiosyncratic little book is not crystal clear, so to speak; it combines the most sublime and poetic prophecy with utterly pragmatic and down-to-earth observation, for example, on the way glass architecture promotes hygiene,

Skidmore, Owings and Merrill: Lever House
New York, 1951.

overcoming the problem of vermin and dirt in dark, dank buildings. In fact, both of our paradigms are ultimately ambiguous: the rationalism of the Crystal Palace is inflected by capitalist surreality and spectacle, while the expressionism of the Crystal Cathedral, born in the apocalyptic atmosphere of World War I Europe, comes to coexist, especially in the work of Mies, for one, with a *sachlich* view of the world. Perhaps it's not surprising that such a paradoxical material as glass should come to thrive on internal contradictions.

Likewise in the work on exhibit, these two impure paradigms of the culture of glass persist, although in even more blurred or merged forms. In

Nicholas Grimshaw's Waterloo International Terminal—painted blue like the Crystal Palace—it is, in fact, the rationalism of computer design that allows for an extraordinarily expressive "organic" form. Nouvel's billboard facade for Cartier operates schizophrenically, outwardly spectacularizing the city while inwardly maintaining the building's privacy and discretion. Tod Williams and Billie Tsien's Phoenix Art Museum Sculpture Pavilion aspires to be a metaphysical space of contemplation while addressing in an ingeniously practical way the climatic problems of a desert building. These complexly negotiated architectural concerns—technical, psychological, environmental—are, it seems to me, what mark these buildings as absolutely contemporary even as they also place the culture of "light construction" within a 150-year-old tradition.

To conclude, I'd like to invoke the Russian tradition of glass architecture—the pre-Constructivist tradition. (Marshall Berman writes beautifully about this in his book *All That Is Solid Melts into Air.*) Fyodor Dostoyevsky went to see the Crystal Palace shortly after it was built. Actually, by the time he saw the building, it had already been moved from Hyde Park to Sydenham Hill, where it was reerected in a more elaborate configuration, one that bears a good deal of resemblance to some of our postmodern shopping malls and suburban office parks. And he hated it. Or at least he dreaded it. Dostoyevsky had been trained as an engineer and architectural draftsman, but he rebelled against this background. He became deeply antipositivist, increasingly suspicious of Western rationalism and materialism. In his book *Notes from the Underground,* the protagonist-narrator rails against a building that you can't throw stones at—that you can't stick your tongue out at, as the character puts it. In part Dostoevsky's novel was a polemic against his contemporary Nikolai Chernyshevsky, who had written a book called *What Is to Be Done?* a year earlier. Chernyshevsky anticipates Le Corbusier's Radiant City by seventy years, describing, through the dream vision of one of his characters, a utopian society whose inhabitants live blissfully in glass towers spaced far apart in acres of greenery. But Dostoyevsky (speaking through his Underground Man) prefers to remain more earth-bound and urban; his character says that a building made of glass is one in which you can never be at home. He declares that it may be fine for engineers to design such buildings, but he remains deeply skeptical about whether it is possible actually to live in one.

With respect to this critique, it's interesting to discover that in late nineteenth-century Russian parlance, the term "Crystal Palace" came to be a synonym for the millennium. The current exhibition at The Museum of Modern Art is suggesting something similar, it seems. In other words, the Crystal Palace will be soon upon us. The question is, can a dematerialized architecture of dazzling surface qualities house our physicality as effectively as our fantasies? And is lightness really an emerging mode of construction—and being—or just an old mode with some new imagery, a past vision of the future? On the threshold of the millennium, we may well throw a few stones at the new palaces and cathedrals.

Joan Ockman is adjunct assistant professor of architecture and director of the Buell Center for the Study of American Architecture at Columbia University's Graduate School of Architecture, Planning and Preservation. A graduate of Harvard University and The Cooper Union School of Architecture, she writes on the history and theory of modern architecture. Besides *Architecture Culture 1943–1968* (Columbia Books of Architecture/Rizzoli International Publications, 1993), Ockman has edited many architectural publications, including *Oppositions*, Oppositions Books and the Revisions series.

JEAN NOUVEL:
CARTIER FOUNDATION

Jean Nouvel's 1994 Cartier Foundation for Contemporary Art project houses both gallery and corporate office space for the reknowned jewelry producer. Located on a highly restrictive site on the Boulevard Raspail in the historic center of Paris. The structure replaces a nineteenth-century villa fronted by a giant cedar originally planted by Chateaubriand. The Cartier project is exemplary of tendencies in architecture toward etherealization and lightness achieved through ambiguity. Nouvel's strategy of dematerialization, a theme that first emerged in his competition entry for the Tête-Défense in Paris (1983), demonstrates a concern for contiguity and interwovenness with the environment. Nouvel creates subtle visual effects that heighten the programmatic dimensions while simultaneously attaining extreme degrees of contextual blending. While parameters of the project's site offered an opportunity to exploit the effects of visual complexity, (for example, in rendering ambiguous whether the historically significant tree is inside or outside of the building) that was arrived at by the architect's conviction that glass is not a matter of transparency but rather of opacity—as the container of refraction. The results of Nouvel's blurring of the difference between inside and outside are documented in the following pages.

Jean Nouvel: Cartier Foundation for Contemporary Art, Paris, 1994. Exterior.

Cartier Foundation for Contemporary Art.
View of exterior.

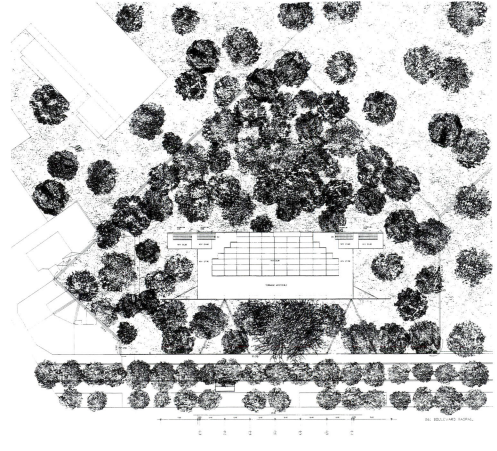

Cartier Foundation for Contemporary Art. Site plan.

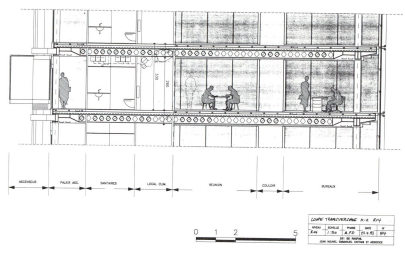

Cartier Foundation for Contemporary Art. section

Cartier Foundation for Contemporary Art
View of exterior.

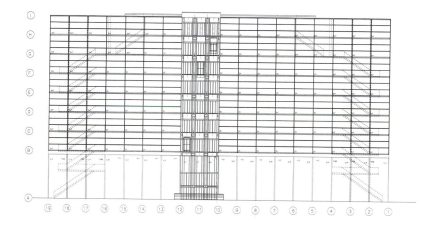

Cartier Foundation for Contemporary Art. Elevation.

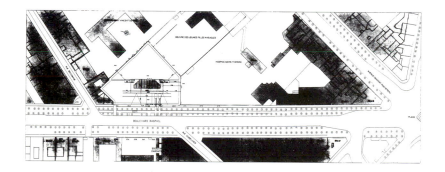

Cartier Foundation of Contemporary Art. Site plan.

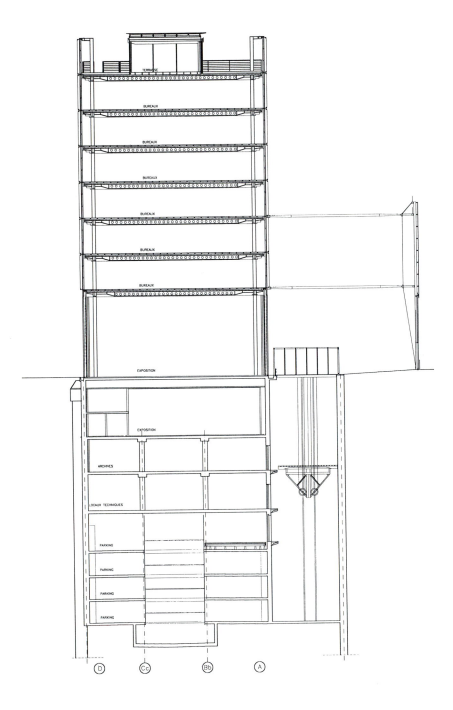

TERRASSE

BUREAUX

BUREAUX

BUREAUX

BUREAUX

BUREAUX

BUREAUX

EXPOSITION

EXPOSITION

ARCHIVES

LOCAUX TECHNIQUES

PARKING

PARKING

PARKING

PARKING

(D) (Cc) (Bb) (A)

Cartier Foundation for Contemporary Art. Section.

Cartier Foundation for Contemporary Art. Exterior/interior view.

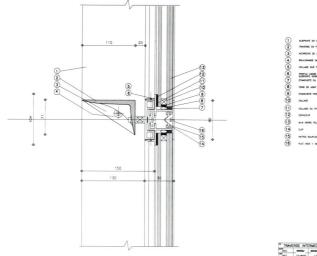

Cartier Foundation for Contemporary Art. Glazing detail.

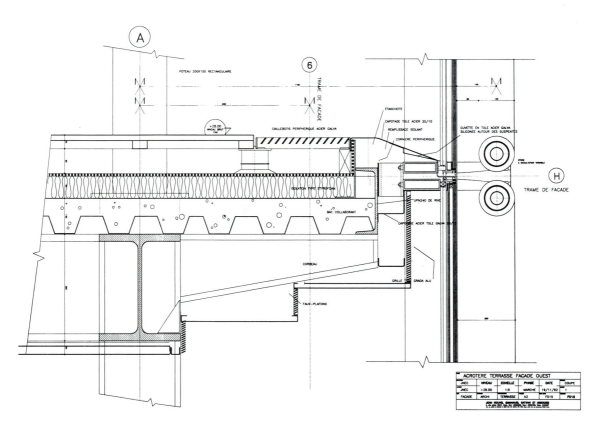

Cartier Foundation for Contemporary Art. Curtain wall detail.

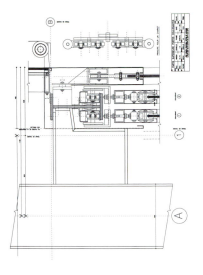

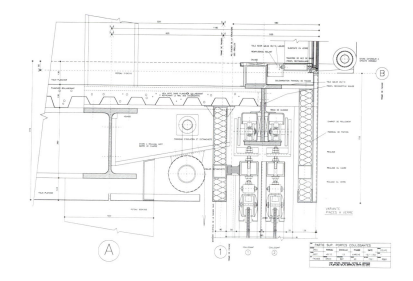

Cartier Foundation for Contemporary Art. Details.

Cartier Foundation for Contemporary Art. View of exterior.

Cartier Foundation for Contemporary Art. View of interior.

Cartier Foundation for Contemporary Art. View of interior.

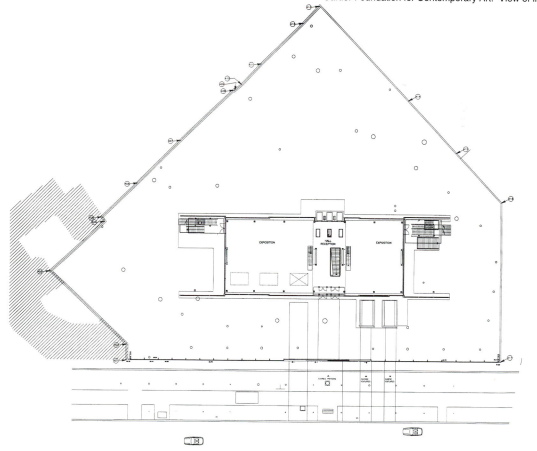

BOULEVARD RASPAIL

Cartier Foundation for Contemporary Art. Plan.

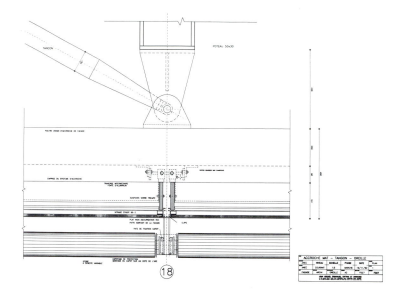

TANGON

POTEAU 50x30

POUTRE 20X20 D'ACCROCHE DE FACADE

EMPRISE DU SYSTEME D'ACCROCHE

TRAVERSE INTERCHARPE
FONCE D'ALLUMINIUM

SUSPENTE VERRE FEUILLETE

VITRAGE STADIP 88-2

PLAT INOX-SECURISATION NEZ
PATTE SORTANT DE LA FACADE

PATTE DE FIXATION CAPOT

CAPOTAGE DE PROTECTION
MONTAGE DU CAPOT SUR UN COTE DE L'AXE

(18)

ACCROCHE MAT - TANGON - OREILLE					
JNEC	NIVEAU	ECHELLE	PHASE	DATE	PLAN
JNEC	COURANT	1:2	MARCHE	19/11/92	1
FACADE	ARCHI	OREILLE	A3	F027	F027

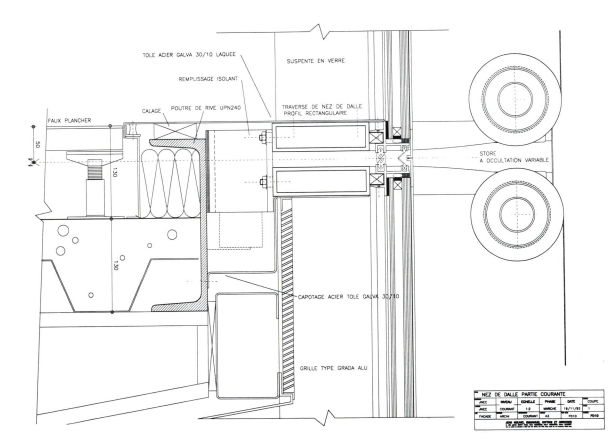

TOLE ACIER GALVA 30/10 LAQUEE

SUSPENTE EN VERRE

REMPLISSAGE ISOLANT

TRAVERSE DE NEZ DE DALLE
PROFIL RECTANGULAIRE

CALAGE   POUTRE DE RIVE UPN240

FAUX PLANCHER

STORE
A OCCULTATION VARIABLE

CAPOTAGE ACIER TOLE GALVA 30/10

GRILLE TYPE GRADA ALU

NEZ DE DALLE PARTIE COURANTE					
JNEC	NIVEAU	ECHELLE	PHASE	DATE	COUPE
JNEC	COURANT	1:2	MARCHE	19/11/92	1
FACADE	ARCHI	COURANT	A3	F010	F010

Cartier Foundation for Contemporary Art. Details.

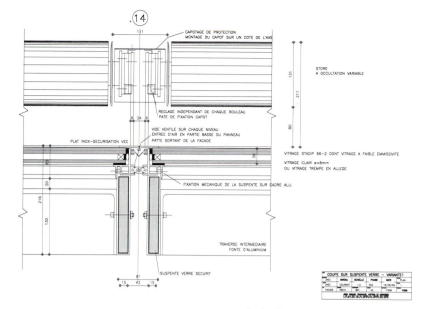

Cartier Foundation for Contemporary Art. Detail.

Cartier Foundation for Contemporary Art. View of exterior.

Cartier Foundation for Contemporary Art. View of exterior.

Cartier Foundation for Contemporary Art. View of interior.

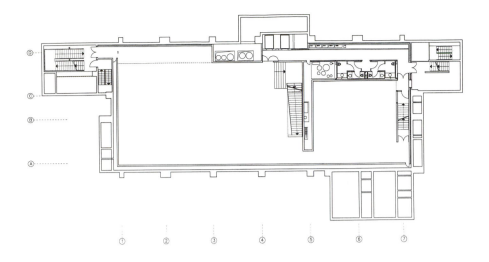

Cartier Foundation for Contemporary Art. Plan.

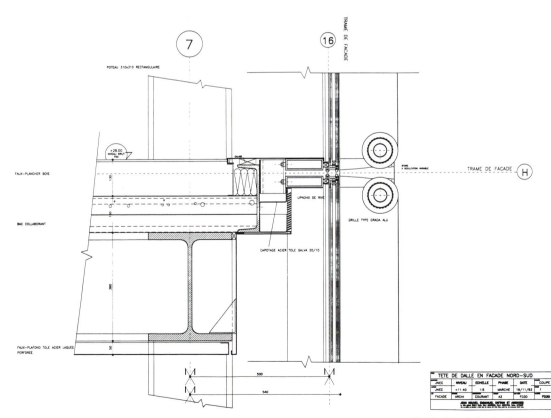

TETE DE DALLE EN FACADE NORD-SUD					
JNEC	NIVEAU	ECHELLE	PHASE	DATE	COUPE
JNEC	+11.40	1:5	MARCHE	19/11/92	1
FACADE	ARCHI	COURANT	A3	F030	F030

Cartier Foundation for Contemporary Art. Details.

Cartier Foundation for Contemporary Art. Elevation.

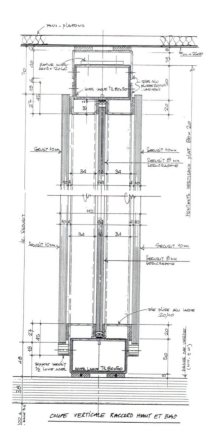

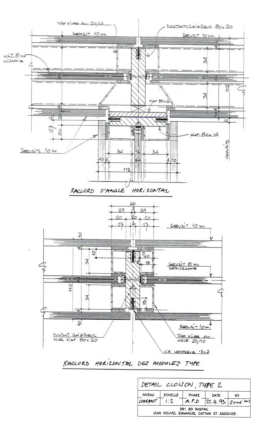

Cartier Foundation for Contemporary Art. Details.

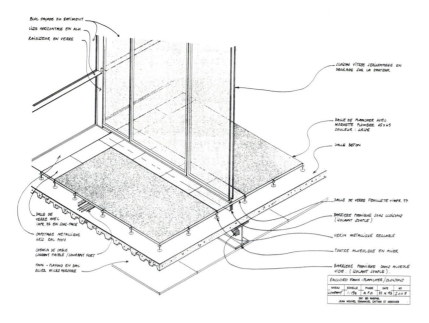

BLOC FACADE DU BATIMENT
LISSE HORIZONTALE EN ALU
RAIDISSEUR EN VERRE

CLOISON VITREE JERIGRAPHIEE EN
DEGRADE SUR LA HAUTEUR

DALLE DE PLANCHER AVEC
MOQUETTE PLOMBEE 65x65
COULEUR : GRISE

DALLE BETON

DALLE DE VERRE FEUILLETE IMPR. 77

BARRIERE PHONIQUE SOUS CLOISONS
(ISOLANT SOUPLE)

VERIN METALLIQUE REGLABLE

POUTRE ALVEOLEE EN ACIER

BARRIERE PHONIQUE DANS ALVEOLE
VIDE. (ISOLANT SOUPLE).

DALLE DE
VERRE AVEC
IMPR. 79 EN SOUS-FACE

CAPOTAGE METALLIQUE
GRIS RAL 7004

CHEMIN DE CABLE
COURANT FAIBLE /COURANT FORT

FAUX - PLAFOND EN BAC
ACIER MICRO PERFORE

RACCORD FAUX-PLANCHER/CLOISONS				
NIVEAU	ECHELLE	PHASE	DATE	N°
COURANT	1:150	A.P.D	22.4.93	2003

281 BD RASPAIL
JEAN NOUVEL EMMANUEL CATTANI ET ASSOCIES

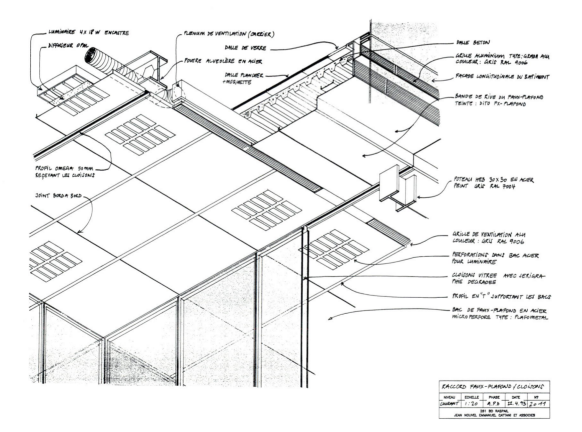

LUMINAIRE 4x18 W ENCASTRE
DIFFUSEUR OPAL

PLENUM DE VENTILATION (CARTIER)
DALLE DE VERRE
POUTRE ALVEOLERE EN ACIER
DALLE PLANCHER
+ MOQUETTE

DALLE BETON

GRILLE ALUMINIUM TYPE:GRADA ALU
COULEUR: GRIS RAL 9006

FACADE LONGITUDINALE DU BATIMENT

BANDE DE RIVE DU FAUX-PLAFOND
TEINTE : DITO FX- PLAFOND

PROFIL OMEGA 50mm
RECEVANT LES CLOISONS

JOINT BORD A BORD

POTEAU HEB 30x30 EN ACIER
PEINT GRIS RAL 7004

GRILLE DE VENTILATION ALU
COULEUR : GRIS RAL 9006

PERFORATIONS DANS BAC ACIER
POUR LUMINAIRE

CLOISONS VITREE AVEC JERIGRA-
PHIE DEGRADEE

PROFIL EN "T" SUPPORTANT LES BACS

BAC DE FAUX-PLAFOND EN ACIER
MICRO PERFORE TYPE : PLAFOMETAL

RACCORD FAUX-PLAFOND / CLOISONS				
NIVEAU	ECHELLE	PHASE	DATE	N°
COURANT	1:20	A.P.D	22.4.93	2011

281 BD RASPAIL
JEAN NOUVEL EMMANUEL CATTANI ET ASSOCIES

Cartier Foundation for Contemporary Art. Floor/ceiling systems.

Cartier Foundation for Contemporary Art. View of exterior.

JACQUES HERZOG AND PIERRE DE MEURON
THREE PROJECTS

Jaques Herzog and Piere de Meuron: Signal Box auf dem Wolf, Basel, 1995. Exterior facade.

Three projects by the design team Jacques Herzog and Pierre de Meuron articulate new developments and possibilities within the architectural facade, or skin.

The six-story Signal Box auf dem wolf, (1995) located in a railyard in Basel is a functional and metaphorical response to the mostly automated building program for coordinating the trains. The entire building is wrapped in strands of twenty-centimeter copper that twist to allow for window openings behind the facade, the effects result in a permeability and depth of surface that seem to invite metaphors of absorption. Given the electronic operations of the project, the woven skin (which also protects the electronic equipment inside) suggests the application of electronic data, as cultural practices become more immersed in information. While the access to functionality in the operable facades of the 1993 SUVA building affords new modes of engagement from the interior, the application of a variety of informational graphics in the 1993 Pfaffenholz Sports Center in St. Louis, where photographic imagery is imprinted upon the inhabitable surfaces of the facade, effects new tangibilities on the exterior.

Top: Signal Box auf dem Wolf. Detail view of exterior.
Bottom: Signal Box auf dem Wolf. View of exterior.

Above Right: Signal Box auf dem Wolf. View of exterior. *Above Middle:* Signal Box auf dem Wolf. Detail view of curtain wall.

Jacques Herzog and Pierre de Meuron: SUVA. alteration of apartment and office building. Basel, Switzerland, 1993. Detail view of exterior.

SUVA alteration of apartment and office building. Basel, Switzerland, 1993. Detail view of exterior.

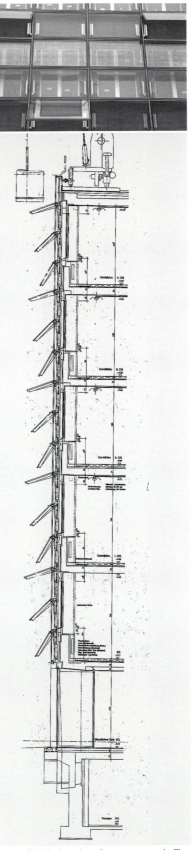

SUVA alteration of apartment and office building. Basel, Switzerland, 1993. Section.

SUVA alteration of apartment and office building. Basel, Switzerland, 1993. Detail view of operable windows.

Jaques Herzog and Piere de Meuron: Pfaffenholz Sports Center, St. Louis, 1993. Detail view of entryway.

Pfaffenholz Sports Center, St. Louis, 1993. Exterior view.

Pfaffenholz Sports Center, St. Louis, 1993. View from interior.

EMERGING COMPLEXITIES

In an attempt to negotiate emergent, multi-disciplinary theories of complex organizational systems within the context of architecture at Columbia University, the School sponsored an all-day symposium during the Spring of 1997 at Avery Hall. Organized by Kunio Kudo and intended as a theoretical adjunct to Jesse Reiser and Nanako Umemoto's Tokyo Studio, the symposium offered a diversity of presentations, responses and general discussions. Presenters were: Akira Asada, Professor of Economics at Kyoto University; Kuniichi Uno, Professor of Literature and Philosophy at Rikkyo University; and Noriaki Kamiya, Professor of Mathematics at Shimane University. In approaching issues of complexity from a variety of positions, thus opening up the material to a discussion of its potential implications for architecture, the presentations established a compelling context to which responses by Sanford Kwinter, Professor of Architecture at Rice University, and Andrew Benjamin, Director of the Centre for Research in Philosophy and Literature at the University of Warwick, were made. Further discussion of topics raised during the symposium was subsequently taken up by Jesse Reiser and Stan Allen, facilitating an open forum on theories of complexity in the context of architecture. Of particular interest was the issue of digital technology and its potential capacity for engendering complex systems of architectural design and production. The panel debated the significance of animation computer software currently in use in many of the advanced design studios at the School. As context for much of the work being done at Columbia, in addition to the Tokyo Studio itself, the symposium effectively provided a necessary interface between the philosophical and theoretical underpinnings essential to a critical study and practice of contemporary architectural design within increasingly complex economic, political and cultural systems of organization.

AKIRA ASADA

The following text is a rereading of the statements made by Akira Asada compiled by Shizaku Moriyama.

While the architectural concept of metabolism can be viewed as essentially grounded in a linear conception of time and growth, wherein both the expression and the experiment are considered part of a fundamentally linear process, "post-metabolism" suggests a non-linear conception of time, that is, the time of the eternal ruin. There are two primary points to be considered: the first refers to a linear, teleological time of growth; the second proposes a model of organic totality. Whereas the work of Kenzo Tange and other metabolists tends to emphasize the former principle, Arata Isozaki, working as a post-metabolist, attempts to escape from the constraints of the metabolist model, entering instead into a more complex, labyrinthine realm of time-space. Metabolism represents architecture and urbanity as mechanical in organization. Post-metabolism, on the other hand, and what has become known as "neo-vitalism," exemplified in the philosophy of Gilles Deleuze, concentrates instead on developing more organic systems capable of dynamic and complex growth. In fact, it might be argued that metabolism is simply a catalyst for modern functionalism, in that it tries to satisfy both a modernist sensibility for logical organization and a more progressive inclination for issues of diversity and complexity. The metabolists, then, conceive of architecture and urbanity as essentially functionalist and yet more complex than what a conventional, modernist scheme might propose. In an attempt to elucidate these points, I will focus primarily on the work of Kenzo Tange and Arata Isozaki, developing a discussion of the differences between metabolism and post-metabolism, with an eventual turn to neo-vitalism and its various permutations in contemporary architectural and urban design.

In 1961 Kenzo Tange's studio proposed a plan for Tokyo Bay that embodied the basic principles of metabolism. The project comprised a spine, or trunk, and an array of branch and leaf elements, which together formed a clear tree-like structure. The use of a tree-like structure as an organizational model, however, proved to be problematic. The metabolists endeavored to develop complex structures yet were always constrained by what was essentially a hierarchical and ultimately simplistic organizational scheme of trunk, branch and leaf components. This model was originally critiqued in Christopher Alexander's 1965 essay "A City is Not a Tree." In that paper, Alexander eloquently demonstrated that no matter how complex such a scheme might appear, it ultimately could be analyzed as a logical, hierarchical organization, the implication being that although the structure looked complex it was, in fact, quite simple in its arrangement.

As opposed to the tree model, Alexander proposed his notion of the "spontaneous city"—a city that forms or grows spontaneously. What he developed was a structural model more akin to that of a lattice than a tree insofar as it was essentially ahierarchical in its organization. When two branch components were divided, for example, they would eventually intersect again, forming a kind of strange loop condition that ultimately returned to the trunk element. The result was a complex, ahierarchical network structure. It is precisely this kind of dichotomy, the tree versus lattice, that would be taken up in a more profound way ten years later by Gilles Deleuze and Felix Guattari in their philosophical writings. The model they used, however, as an example of a complex, ahierarchical

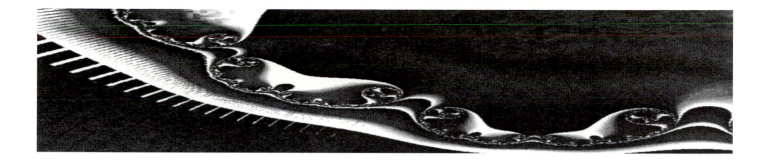

system, is that of the rhizome. The metabolists were conscious of these critiques and yet were incapable of rethinking their basic architectural model. Alexander's paper was even translated into Japanese in 1967, though it is obvious it never had a lasting effect, in that Tange and his colleagues continued to rely on hierarchical models of organization.

At this point I would like to turn to the work of Arata Isozaki, who I will suggest acted as a post-metabolist. Although his early project "City in the Air," designed in 1961, appears at first glance to be a tree structure, one notices on closer inspection that it is much more like a forest of tree structures. Isozaki developed a system of urban intersections and interconnections in the air, ultimately providing for a grand forest-like labyrinth structure supported by infrastructural trunk elements that also afforded commercial and residential program "plug-ins" like those found in Peter Cook's 1964 "Plug-in City."

Isozaki further challenged conventional methods of metabolism through an experimental exhibition held in Tokyo in which he projected a map of Tokyo onto a table. Providing hammers, nails and wires, Isozaki then encouraged the audience to engage with the experiment by setting up a network of nails and wire. Nails served to signify "infrastructural nodes," with the wire strung between them representing office or residential complexes in the air. Isozaki successfully empowered the audience with the ability to design through a dynamic, interactive and ultimately, collective process. The final results were really quite stunning, with wire traveling not only from nail to nail but extending as well to the walls, ceiling and adjacent exhibition spaces. The model had become truly complex, suggesting a rhizomatic city of ahierarchical networks of infrastructure and program. Already Isozaki had initiated a critical development in the metabolist's project, suggesting, perhaps for the first time, the potential for real urban and architectural complexity.

Real complexity, then, is possible only when it is liberated from conventional notions of organic totality. Moving beyond the biomorphic model toward a more natural or even semi-autonomous one, as the exhibition experiment demonstrated, whereby the sovereignty of the individual designer or creator is opened up to an array of external forces and interventions, Isozaki emphasized the need to consider diverse and numerous forces in order to foster true complexity. Complexity is possible only when it is liberated from linear teleological time. Without such liberation there can be no potential for real emergence, dissipation and density.

In the mid-1960s, due primarily to the advent of information technology, the focus of architecture shifted from a conception of complexity viewed in terms of a biological model to one of information. This shift was registered not only in the work of Isozaki but in that of many of his contemporaries, including Archigram, Superstudio and Archizoom. They arrived at a concept of open or virtual architecture consistent with the conditions of informational network systems or cybernetic environments. These and other practices were negotiating both the physicality of megastructure and the virtuality of an "informatic" network, an approach that can still be seen today in the work of architects Rem Koolhaas and Bernard Tschumi, whose

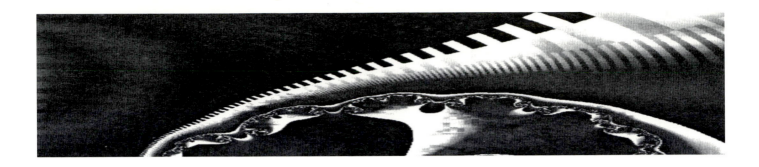

respective theories of "bigness" and "event-space" seem particularly relevant to a discussion of the actual and the virtual.

In considering "light construction," for example, as conceived in the Museum of Modern Art's 1995 exhibition of the same name, what is really of interest is not a reading of lightness in terms of gravity, but the translucency of the architectural membrane as an interface for informational exchange. In 1968 Archigram proposed the speculative project "Instant City," which proposed a temporary and mobile event-space, emphasizing temporality and virtuality. Likewise, Superstudio's "Continuous Monument" of 1969 proposes a structure so big that the entire space becomes an endless interior in which the emphasis shifts from architecture to information.

More recently, Isozaki's proposal for the Chinese government for a man-made island approximately the size of the city of Venice has raised similar issues. Isozaki's interest in the distribution of churches in Venice as a starting point for the development of the project, for example, suggests a preoccupation with a fabricated origin. He goes further to provide a program of

artificial life deriving from computer simulation software, such that the points move around one another with varying degrees of random disturbance and interference. Eventually certain points approach sets of other points, forming a piazza-like configuration. As with his Tokyo exhibition experiment, in which Isozaki integrated the participation of the audience into the design process, the Venice project provokes intervention from outside participants that is effected via the Internet. These incursions likewise affect the course of what essentially has become a system of autopoeitic morphogenesis. Unlike the Tokyo experiment, however, in which Isozaki was limited to hammers, nails and wires in developing a complex, semi-autonomous and interactive design process, the Venice project utilizes contemporary technological advancements and information network design to propel the design process. In some cases, for example, Isozaki invited as many as 100 artists and architects from around the world to collaborate on the various sections of the Venice/Tokyo project. In a sense, Isozaki had returned to post-metabolism by way of contemporary information technologies, developing a complex

and intriguing simultaneity of autopoeitic and allopoeitic processes.

More recently, in terms of architectural theory, we have begun to see what can be called a "new vitalism" in the work of Henri Bergson and that of Gilles Deleuze and Felix Guattari and in emerging models of nonlinear, fluid-dynamic morphogenesis. Although these developments are serving to open up numerous possibilities for a morphogenetic system liberated from the governing constraints of a single author or telos, what is of concern is the regression of returning to the failed vitalism of both the nineteenth century and the 1960s.

Essentially a philosophy of complexity, DeleuzioGuattarian thought negotiates not only the actual realm but the virtual one as well. In fact, one might argue that the primary intention of Deleuzian philosophy is that of establishing a theory of the virtual. Today there is extensive discussion of what is referred to as virtual reality. According to Deleuze and Guattari, however, virtual reality is nothing but an illusionary, technological phenomenon. Just as architecture is governed by gravity in this world,

it might, in a certain possible world, in a digital environment for example, transgress the limitations of gravity, thus developing entirely new spatial conditions.

This raises the question of the virtual. In DeleuzioGuattarian thought, as unrealized possibilities are simply discarded, the virtual, nevertheless, manages to retain its reality. For instance, if we believe that access to the virtual world exists somewhere other than in this reality, we again fall into a familiar idealistic trap. The most important point of DeleuzioGuattarian philosophy is its emphasis on the individual crystal present in the here and now, that which can be defined as a kind of short circuit to both the actual and the virtual. It is a process of oscillation between an actual dimension and a virtual one. In the virtual dimension the virtual itself does not exist elsewhere. For example, in Cézanne's painting one often finds what could be considered a relatively poor depiction of landscape in terms of reality. Virtually, however, it is vibrant and rich in color and vibration. In a sense, then, the actual and virtual somehow co-exist through a state of perpetual oscillation.

Viewed in terms of Bergson's philosophy, the crystal corresponds to the present, whose counterpart is the past, indicating that the past is indeed not close at all. Rather, the past is preserved in a state of virtuality. In DeleuzioGuattarian philosophy one observes the crystal, or the visual, as that which is oscillating between the here and now, and the now and here. Additionally, one notices the purely virtual through which everything *is*, in a sense, actualized or differentiated.

I am in agreement with Deleuze and Guattari when they write about the crystal and its peculiar capacity to oscillate between the virtual and the actual. I wonder, however, if this Deleuzian ontology of the virtual doesn't run the risk of falling into an ideological trap. Deleuze was aware of the difficulty, if not the impossibility, of completing his philosophical system and as a result decided to work with Felix Guattari, the great non-philosopher. Guattari functioned as a connector, linking Deleuzian philosophy with numerous academic fields and effectively setting up compelling dialogues with disciplines as diverse as architecture, art, psychology and politics.

What is important about the morphogenetic model is the degree to which it allows for a coexistence of various forces, engendering an autogenetic or autopoeitic system. Autopoeitic systems produce theories of complex self-organization that nevertheless can become very problematic. It is possible to argue, for example, that these new models are in fact nothing more than a new and more sophisticated version of the Christian philosophy of the self as generative of itself as well as its non-self. Self-organization or autopoeisis is thus impossible without the necessary random influx of external forces. This is precisely Guattari's point when he talks about the machine and its arrangement—that a machinic arrangement of heterogeneous forces and heterogeneous autopoeitic processes are much more interesting than simple models of poeisis.

In conclusion, there is an important dilemma for architecture that I would term the "stopping problem." Computer modeling, for example, can be transformed endlessly, but in reality we are ultimately forced to freeze a form at a certain moment in order to make architecture. This, in a sense,

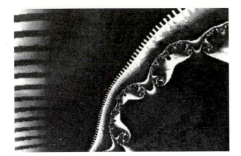

becomes an extremely political moment in time, one when external forces intervene in the process. Without consideration of the stopping of forces engaged in the design process, the temporal and transformative nature of the study is potentially lost. There is, nevertheless, a problem when dynamic, animated architectural projects are suddenly frozen and limited to a single frame. In other words, even if the actual image should somehow be fixed and stopped, it seems that one must, in effect, separate the image from the virtual information. This would be the real definition of the virtual. The actual image, even when stopped, is nevertheless accompanied by the virtual image. In this sense the image never stops moving virtually. The translation of this dynamic seems to be the real challenge confronting designers and artists today.

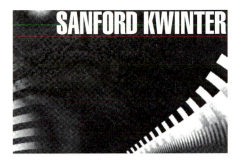

A MATERIALISM OF THE INCORPOREAL

One of the signal problems of the design world, of contemporary design epistemology one might even say, is the function and significance of the diagram. After World War II, as is commonly known, an extraordinary increase in the belief and application of science and engineering to everyday life took place. This was accompanied by a growing application and deployment of invisible material logics, both to explain and to generate reality. It bears pointing out, even at the cost of excessive simplification, that the advent of controlled nuclear processes, microwave and radar-signal processing, industrial applications of synthetic chemistry, ballistics and cryptology were made possible almost entirely by theoretical and practical advances in information science. Industrial societies became increasingly saturated with these new embedded logics and the corresponding motor habits that they produced, but they became subjugated by them—invisibly— according to what one might call a "subtle coup." The diagram is now very usefully understood as informational. Today the sciences of complexity give us the most useful understanding of the dynamic, algorithmic nature of diagrams.

Yet to what do we refer when we use the term "complexity"? Does complexity actually refer to something real, or is it merely a new chimera or screen through which physical reality is filtered, and which gives rise to a spate of only apparently new problems that are not real problems at all because they cannot be answered in classically scientific or even design terms? Such philosophical/ epistemological skepticism is not unwarranted, and yet, it is very often misplaced. Akira Asada has expressed some of this same skepticism, most of which can be eliminated by placing the complexity problem in a broader and more detailed philosophical and historical context.

Complexity theory can be said to target three primary phenomena in the natural and the non-natural world: the phenomena of integration, organization and coordination. These phenomena undeniably exist in the world, but science has never been able to interrogate them in its customary numerical or "hard" terms.

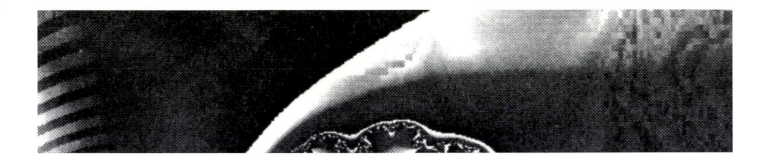

Philosophy has always had to step in, along with some makeshift methods in the social sciences and occasionally aesthetics. When we, today, inquire into the nature and activity of design processes (spontaneous and natural, or human and contrived), we are asking: "When something appears, what agencies are responsible for giving this particular shape to this particular appearance?" Complexity theory, or dynamical systems theory, is seeking to reconfigure the answer to this question by positing the perpetual interaction of moving, evolving systems: one invisible (the diagram) and one visible (the real). The primary phenomena studied by the new sciences are actually visible to, or intuitable by, a living observer, but not to a non-living one, say, to a camera or a measuring device. How, for example, can the phenomenon of integration be identified or located? To explain the problem, let me simplify greatly by limiting it to a figure/ground example. An active ground, one can say, poses a continual threat to the figure upon or within it unless that figure is itself active and flexible; is in continual communication with the ground through feedback loops moving in both directions; and constitutes

within itself a system of even greater density of correlations and exchanges so that it can throw up a boundary of order, or a discontinuity between itself and the world that surrounds it. The figure integrates its surroundings the way a lens focuses and intensifies ambient light, butit also integrates the differential events in the ambient environment (the changes) that function as a kind of motor for it, a thermodynamic potential to be tapped.

The next phenomenon under consideration is that of organization. Organization played a central role in the life sciences in the 1920s and 1930s and then again in the 1960s, addressing the philosophical impasses that still lingered from the older mechanist-vitalist debates. The task of the organization concept was to explain differentiation, dissymmetry and specialization in the development of a form, because by the 1920s biologists had already abandoned the idea of a direct "readout theory" of genetic diagrams. Organization relies on the notion of pattern; it attempts to explain how pattern can arise uniquely through internal controls, and how these control factors sustain themselves, take on a direction and then

assume the appearance of autonomy, or life. The concept of organization targets primarily the emergence of sequenced events as the source of developmental mechanics and formal stability. If organization explains differentiation (novelty) and stability (persistence in being), then the third term I am positing—coordination—explains how things actually move, how they "transition" smoothly, even gracefully between many states, how they emit temporal, rhythmic morphologies or coherent behaviors.

Integration, organization and coordination are each abstract nouns without demonstrable correlates in the physical or chemical world. Yet this does not mean that they are immaterial, (far from it!) only that they are incorporeal. Their materiality quite simply is not manifested in space but rather in time.

These three phenomena that I have identified with complexity models can all be grouped under a larger rubric that Henri Bergson referred to as "duration." Complexity is the science of the materialism—or the materialization—of time. This then comes back to the problem of the virtual as it was touched on by

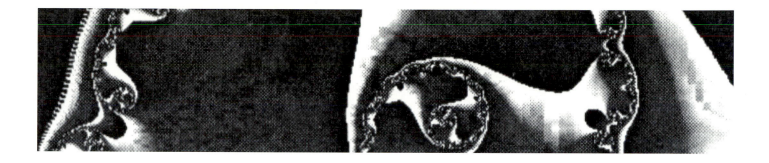

Asada. There is, of course, a lot of talk today around the problem of virtuality, though I don't mean virtuality simply in the trivial sense of objects in synthetic sensory environments. In Bergsonian and Deleuzian ontology, virtuality plays an important role in explaining the problem of appearance in the world itself and the forces that manifest through it. According to this ontology (developed primarily in Gilles Deleuze's *Difference and Repetition*), a critical distinction is indeed maintained, as Asada points out, between two models of morphogenesis, between two axes or models of appearance. On the one hand, there is the Possible-Real axis, and on the other, the axis of the Virtual-Actual. Of course to speak of a Bergsonian-Deleuzian ontology in the first place is to presuppose a set of common principles in the two systems. I will suggest just two here: the idea that Being is the expression of a fundamental mobility; and that there are two types of difference—those that appear in space and those that appear in time—but that only the type that appears in time is *real*.

What exists around us is actual. But according to what template or diagram does this expressed world manifest itself? According to the Possible-Real model, everything real is the expression of a Possible that preceded it, that was identical to it, and that was fully pre-given. Reality, according to this model, is a mere selection of images prepared in advance. This is the type of pseudo- or mechanistic diagrammatism that one today wishes to avoid. The principle of selection guarantees that only one version of reality will appear; while another process of limitation assures that the process of realization/expression will take place in successive stages rather than all at once. This latter principle (limitation) might appear to constitute a time principle, though in fact it does so only in the most mechanical, external and abstract sense: reality would be nothing but a picture of possibility repeated (this is the bad repetition, the pseudo-diagram), and the world of possibility would be nothing more than an unchanging storehouse of images existing from time immemorial. The world here is always already formed and given in advance, a dead mechanical object. Bergson believed this to be the fundamental fallacy of Western metaphysics: the idea that there exists a "realm of possibility" underlying the world of actuality.

His so-called "ontologization" of the virtual belongs to his project of freeing the diagram and its becoming from its metaphysical basis to establish a neo-materialist basis for time.

The virtual—we are told—is real, even if it is not yet actual. What does this mean? The virtual is related to the actual, not by a transposition—a becoming real—but by a transformation through integration, organization and coordination. The virtual is real because it exists in this reality as a free difference, not yet combined with other differences and lodged in a salient form. The virtual is linked to the actual through a developmental passage from one state to another, one in which the free difference is incarnated or assembled. It passes from one moment-event in order to emerge later—differently, uniquely—within another. The actual does not resemble the virtual (as the real does the possible); its rule is rather one of difference, innovation or creation. Actualization is differentiation because it occurs in time and with time. Every moment represents a successive individuation-differentiation of matter from the state that preceded it. Actualization is the free

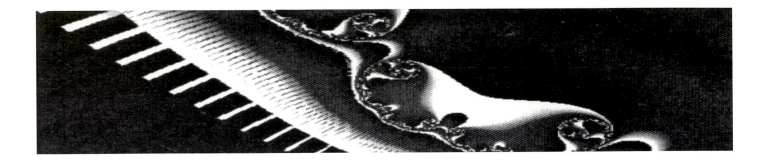

movement, the capture and the materialization of difference. Reality becomes a flow—an irreducible actualizing duration that inflects, combines and separates—that leaves nothing untransformed.

Every thing is given, and arrives, in time. Its qualities, its affects and its structure may be apprehended in space, but in adopting this posture we are already breaking the world into abstractions. In time, and only in time, do matter and world reveal themselves. In other words, time is real.

To acknowledge that the world is the product of actualization processes—the exfoliation of diagrams—is to acknowledge that time, on its own, is both productive and concrete. It does not follow that this set of notions necessarily leads to an untenable or naive vitalism. As Bergson said, "Reality makes or remakes itself, but it is never something made." This clear rejection of any external agency in the unfolding of things is unambiguous evidence that Bergson was more of a "neo-vitalist" than a classical, or metaphysical vitalist of the nineteenth-century type. In other words, Bergson was a thinker of immanent, rather transcendent

causes. This means his system sought to explain reality in the same terms in which reality is given, without having recourse to "extra" principles that come, like divine endowments, from outside the real itself. Thus the ultimate question, from an ontological perspective, would seem to be, "Why is the universe creative, rather than not, and why is it so despite the high cost of creation (negentropy)?" But of course this question is already neo-vitalist before we have even begun. The question is neo-vitalist for the simple reason that we presuppose that the universe is driven, that it moves, integrates—that it is alive. Indeed it is not even necessary to posit aliveness–merely the qualities of drivenness, movement and integration—three of the primary tenets of form theory in the life sciences, or complexity theory.

It has been claimed by one complexity theorist that "all complexity moves toward biology," and this is no trivial assertion. Indeed complexity is the movement toward biology. It marks the transition where communication, control and pattern formation, or relationships of information, take over in an organized substrate from

relationships of energy. Historically, this movement—the emergence of what I like to call a "bio-logic"—began with the nineteenth century's science of heat (thermodynamics) as the study of ineluctable transitions (cold to hot, order to disorder, difference to homogeneity) and the theory of evolution (the homogeneous and simple to the differentiated and the complex). The life sciences could not fully emerge on an independent basis until a theoretical—mathematical basis could be provided for them. Physics itself had to become an "information" science before biology could emerge gradually to supplant it. (This history extends from Ludwig Boltzmann's statistical theory of gases to the postwar era's elaborations by Norbert Weiner, Claude Shannon, Alan Turing and John von Neumann.) Such a view of history makes it very difficult to accept Asada's position, or the general position in Japanese architecture and thought today, that wishes to see "informatics" as a new or independent development in the history of ideas and aesthetics, as a putative "third stage" following and supplanting the physics model and biology models. What I call the bio-logic is the informational paradigm par

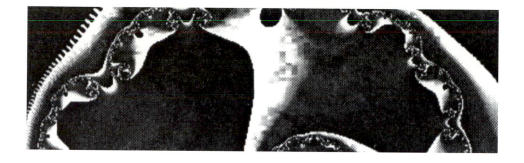

excellence. To speak about "invisible" architectures and informational networks, to invoke "dematerialization" processes in their support, is to misunderstand the problem. It is to mistake the incorporeal for the immaterial, and to mistake the virtual for the phantom real.

Informational architectures were at the heart of American aesthetics since the 1960s (Robert Smithson is an important example), but the advent of electronic gadgetry and the emergence of an over-developed communications infrastructure has not changed the fundamental problem one iota. Our problem today remains one of freeing ourselves from the impoverishments of mechanism (or in the case of some contemporary Japanese tendencies, of "neo-mechanism") through the actualization or incarnation of "free" or invisible difference, that is, of virtuality, through the relentless invention of techniques whose task is to materialize the incorporeal by embedding everything in the flow of time. In time everything is related; and it is this multiplicity of relations, both their shifting and mobile nature and the imperturbable unity of the medium in which they move (time,

duration), to which the study of complexity—or, as Bergson called it, the science of intuition—responds. Architecture plays, or could and should play, a privileged role in bringing these processes of organization, integration and coordination not only to the foreground of public and cultural appearance but also to the more subtle arena of experience itself, to the place where the time of things and the time of the body are one, to the space of intuition. Through the materialization of actualization, architecture has the capacity to free the imagination from three-dimensional experience—to free it from the curse of so-called "invisible processes" and hidden diagrams and to show us that the processes and events which give form to our world and our lives have shapes of their own.

L'INFORME QUI FORME: BATAILLE, DELEUZE AND ARCHITECTURE

Writing about poetry, writing of it within a "digression" on poetry, writing in a way that, on the level of content, causes a confrontation with authenticity and thus with having to allow for the possibility of there being an authentic poetry, Georges Bataille stages an encounter with architecture that will work to undo his own famous entry in *Dictionnaire critique*.[1] While poetry may appear to be distanced from the reality of architecture, it remains the case that within Bataille's digression the two touch because his concern with poetry becomes a concern with the presence of form, though more significantly with the generation of form. It is for this reason that texts ostensibly on architecture—and here this will involve both the text *"Architecture"* as well as *"L'obélisque," "Le labyrinthe"* and *"Muse"*—will need to be distanced from a concern with the architectural once the architectural is understood as a problem of the generation of form. The texts on buildings and monuments that occur within Bataille's writings raise a different though related problem.[2] What

emerges from an analysis of those texts is the question of the extent to which such a site—the monument or building—can be sustained as the locus of counter investments, perhaps even of symbolic reworkings. What this means is that the building is viewed as having a symbolic dimension and it is this symbolic dimension that determines the building's meaning. To operate on the level of meaning—the building as sign—is to defer ostensibly architectural questions, since when the symbolic is made central any attempt to connect signification and form is deferred. Signification can only be primary once the generation of form has been granted centrality.

It is the centrality of the symbolic, and thus of the attempt to strip the symbolic of its power, that governs the "sacrilege" enacted by Simone as an integral part of her confession taking place within the *récit* "The Story of The Eye." Masturbating within the confessional is an affront to the site. The complicity of the priest reworks the site. However, even though its symbolic determinations may have been checked by the affirmation of a form of auto-eroticism, the architecture is left untouched. In other words, masturbation and the

inexorable slide toward eroticism do not engage with form and thus with the architectural problem of the interrelationship between form and program. Within the confines of the *récit* form is only an appearance and thus the bearer of meaning. Indeed, the question of form as the continual place of a repositioning and thus of a reworking or redescription plays an integral role with that text. Sir Edmond's own redescription of the elements of the Eucharist will hold form in place. Form can be reformed, while what is removed from consideration is the question of form:

> ...the wafers...are nothing other than the sperm of Christ in the form of *(sous forme de)* a small white cake. (vol. 1. p. 63.)

What this means in this instance is that architecture—the architecture of the church—like the wafers, endures without any consideration being given either to the nature of form or to its production. Hence, it could be conjectured that there is no real confrontation with the architectural but only with signification. Form, once understood as effectively present, cannot escape its already having been linked to the presence of the

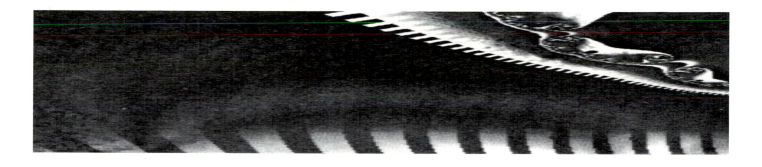

symbolic. Within architecture this can be provisionally understood as the presence of program. In Bataille's formulation, however, rather than that formulation staging the interarticulation of program and form, they have been separated. This means that architecture comes to be abandoned as a concern in the texts that take architecture as the ostensible object of analysis. The argument here is that the problems inherent in Bataille's encounter with the architectural provide the locus within which it will become possible to situate, albeit critically, the architectural imperative emerging from Gilles Deleuze's writing on the "fold" and from the way in which Deleuze distinguishes between smooth and striated space in *A Thousand Plateaus.*

In *Inner Experience* Bataille, in his digression on poetry, defines poetry as the move from the known to the unknown. The sacrifice of both the referent and the conventions and expectations of usage occur in a relentless drive toward the yet-to-be-defined. This is the space of the literary. Sacrifice, and thus poetry, are opposed within Bataille's writings to the law, to morality, in sum to what he describes as "project."

And yet the opposition is not absolute; whatever it is that is marked out by terms such as "sacrifice," "ecstasy," "nudity" and so forth, will be operative and thus present as workful within the presentation of work. Each resists the possibility of a simple reduction to the literal. Poetry understood as the negative, the power of the unknown, demanding to be maintained as the unknown and thus as the always-to-be-defined, will insist on—also within—its own presentation and its being present within words, within the very words that are the place of "project." Bataille articulates this position with disarming clarity:

> The plan of the moral is the plan of the project. The contrary to project is sacrifice. Sacrifice takes on the forms of project. *(tombe dans les formes du projet)* but in appearance only... (vol. 5, p. 158)

These two moments, working with a concern for the literary, reach beyond themselves. They call attention to that which works with the possibility of presentation itself: presence as form. In such a context this has two direct consequences. The first is the impossibility of pure destruction, the nihilistic gesture

that is also found in the promulgation of complete fragmentation (the critique of unity as the positing of a literal *disjecta membra*). Equally, however, it opens up the possibility of defining alterity in terms of an engagement with appearance. The questions arising with these consequences not only concern what is meant by appearance but whether or not the presence of poetry or sacrifice mediates appearance. In the latter case, appearance would no longer be merely appearance. It is the possibility of this mediation, and thus for appearance to bear the mark of the power of the negative—a setup described by Maurice Blanchot as the struggle that marks the inception of any work—that is at its most exacting within architecture because of the way in which architecture is present.[3]

As has already been intimated, Bataille's recognition of the necessary retention of words, of order, of syntax and sentences, needs to be understood initially as a defiant stand against nihilism. However, for Bataille's own undertaking to be successful, this can be the only sense given to appearance. When he writes of *"les formes du projet,"* there is

only one sense in which poetry can have this quality. Again, the word *form* will engender the same problem. What must be argued is that neither appearance nor form are either appearance or form, if the latter are understood as surface effects. Rather, they denote the presence of an elementary materiality—words and their sustained unfolding. Indeed it is at this precise point that it becomes possible to identify not the meaning of Bataille's writings but their signification, the latter being the relation that the writings have to their own material presence. Both as a book and as writing, *Inner Experience (L'expérience intérieure)* works to escape the opposition of appearance and depth by producing from within itself the very openings, fissures, delays and thus experiences that it attempts to present. Its singularity is to be located at that precise point. Its own limits are the limits of its appearance. Neither on the level of form nor of appearance does *Inner Experience* appear as a book, or work within the tradition of writing, despite its being a book and the work of writing.

What appears therefore cannot automatically be incorporated into a straightforward distinction between surface and depth. This position has significant consequences. The insistence on materiality means that the claim concerning appearance cannot be generalized. It will already have been marked by an ineliminable specificity. What this entails is that appearance and form become almost local concerns. What becomes fundamental is allowing for the distinction between "the form of project" and "project," and thus between poetry and sacrifice on the one hand, and, mere appearance on the other. Here, this distinction will have to be thought in terms of its already involving a productive overlapping.

Even though the way such a distinction will work within the practices of philosophy and architecture will always involve nuanced decisions and fragile openings, it remains that the distinction between "the form of project" and "project" is not to be understood as a simple either/or. Working with their necessarily imbricated presence means, in the first place, insisting on the force of materiality, and second, allowing for the particular nature of the distinction to be generated by the work's work; in other words, by its own self-generating and therefore self-effecting process of realization. It will also involve recognizing that the work of the negative, what can be identified as a productive negativity, will have a certain immateriality. Raising the possibility of an immaterial presence is not intended to introduce a transcendental element into architecture. Rather, once it is no longer possible to locate the excessive—understood as that which in being in excess of function has a transformative effect on the nature of function—within an element, aspect or part of the building, then, even though the presence of the excessive will have material consequences, they will have been produced by that which is immaterially present. It will be essential to return to this form of immateriality.

The presence of a process of realization yields economies. In the same way that there will be an important distinction made between the pure affirmation of the interplay of poetry and project and the simple presence of project, it will have to be possible to distinguish between an architecture of project and one in which there is a sustained negotiation with the question of appearance. An architecture of project can be

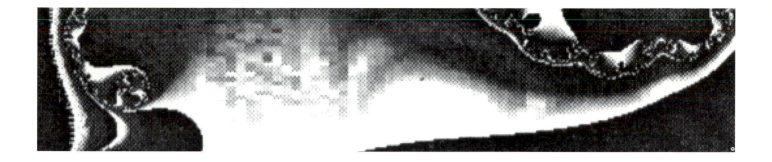

defined as oscillating between the form-follows-function of conventional modernism and the apparent indifference between form and function characterizing much postmodernist architecture. As such there is the impossibility of pure generality, in the precise manner that it is impossible to conceive of architecture *tout court*. A lacking of generality is linked to the question of the essence. What this means is that rather than allocating to the essence a possible determination that is on the one hand unified in nature, while on the other withdrawn from the domain of facticity, the essential will become the setting of architectures that are always determined by preexisting constraints. What constrains architecture—the inescapable reciprocity between shelter and the sheltered, a reciprocity that is itself only thinkable within particularity—will be essential to architecture being what it is. The way constraints are instantiated becomes the necessary localization of the architectural, its particularity as already determined by function and program. The two working together—the constraint of architecture having to function and the formal presence interarticulated with that function—will continue to

yield that which is essential to an architectural practice. What this yields is a setup that is marked by an insistent irreducibility. It is an irreducibility that is marked by a complex series of interconnections. In the first place, it is the interconnection between dominance and the constraint of function. In the second, it is the link between criticality and its necessary interconnection with a function that is only maintained within the possibility of its being transformed. Since what is at stake is an ineliminable irreducibility, what is demanded is judgment. Judgment does not emerge for ethical reasons. The demand for judgment arises because of an opening necessitating a decision. In broad terms, what this amounts to is the claim that what is essential to architecture is that which will always allow for the divide that is at work within Bataille's construal of the distinction between poetry and project.

It is this setup that needs to be opposed to the formulation given to architecture in the famous entry in *Dictionnaire critique*. Leaving aside Bataille's Vitruvian conjoining of architecture and the body, what endures as central is the construal of form. In this specific context

Bataille raises the question of form in the following way:

> It is in the form of *(c'est sous la forme des)* cathedrals and palaces that the state address itself to and imposes silence on the multitudes. (vol. 1, p. 170)

It is in these terms that he situates the storming of the Bastille. What is fundamental to this formulation is the role attributed to the symbolic presence of buildings and thus to their presence as monuments rather than as the ostensibly architectural. Form only occurs in this formulation in terms of providing the symbol: *"c'est sous la forme ... ."* What this establishes is a distinction between a conception of form that is symbolic, and thus works as a monument, and form that is emergent, and thus demands to be understood in terms of that which generated it. In sum, it is as though form is held within a distinction between building and monument on one side and architecture on the other.

Bataille writes,

> The taking of the Bastille is symbolic of this state of things: it is difficult to explain the movement of the crowd, other

than by the animosity of the people against the monuments that are veritable masters. (vol 1, p. 170)

The taking of the Bastille is linked, necessarily, to the symbolic presence of the Bastille. The Bastille was construed as a monument. The struggle was against the specificity of its monumentality. The link between the monument understood as a building and architecture becomes a particular problem that cannot be addressed by equating each of the elements within this complex formulation.

Once it becomes possible to consider the production form as that which is produced, rather than linking architecture to monumentality—a linkage in which architecture, in the guise of building, runs the real risk of being condemned as necessarily oppressive—it becomes imperative to link that movement to Bataille's own conception of a productive negativity. Form will need to be connected to another type of production. The important point here will be that criticality, as shall be suggested, does not reside in a didactic architecture but in the interarticulated copresence of the material and the immaterial. The immaterial brings with it the work of the negative. Holding to the *im*, holding to it beyond the hold of the logic of negation, holding its negativity as productive, will open up the possibility of reworking the possibility of alterity within architecture. The stimulus comes not from Bataille's work on architecture itself, but from texts taking as central the problem of the generation of form. As such, what will emerge is what can be described as *l'informe qui forme*.[4]

Initially published in *Documents*, and again in the *Dictionnaire*, this short work, just thirteen lines long in volume 1 of Bataille's *Oeuvres complètes*, touches on the issues central to the architectural. Rather than pretending to offer an exhaustive commentary on this text, a number of key moments will be pursued. In the first instance Bataille describes *"l'informe"* as

> a term serving to declassify the general exigency that each thing has its form. (vol.1, p. 217)

The key here is the process identified by the term "declassify." The second moment has to do with the other demand that *"l'informe"* brings with it. It is signaled by the claim that "it would be necessary, in effect for academic men to be content, that the universe take form." For Bataille the project of philosophy—perhaps philosophy as project—is ineliminably linked to establishing and maintaining form. The final point, and it could be argued that it is a point that reiterates the movement of declassifying, is that responding to this setup involves neither destruction nor the positing of the utopian but a counter affirmation: "...affirming that the universe resembles nothing and is only *l'informe* comes back to saying that the universe is something like a spider or spit." The last point is the most revealing. It constitutes the moment at which, it could be argued, Bataille comes to misrepresent *l'informe* by seeking to represent it. Or rather, in representing it, in literalizing it, its structuring force is betrayed. It will be this problem that opens up the architectural impulse within Deleuze's conception of the fold, and thus also of space. Prior to addressing Deleuze, it is essential to remain with *l'informe*.

Perhaps the greatest temptation is to consider *l'informe* as the simple opposite of *la forme*. Opposition here would mean that whatever

pertained to one would necessarily not pertain to the other. While it appears to be only a philosophical concern and not an architectural one, the central question here is how the *in* of *l'informe* is to be understood. Despite the gesture toward the philosophical, this is also the central architectural question. One possible way of understanding the *in* is as a negation that allows for its own negation. The move to form would occur with the negation of *l'informe*. However, when Bataille suggests that one of the functions of *l'informe* is to bring about a change in register and thus reposition the exigency linked to form, part of that process will be the distancing of the opposition between *forme* and *l'informe* understood as a mutually excluding either/or. What reemerges at this precise point is the analogy with poetry. Poetry sustains language. It works with words, meanings, syntax and so forth, all of which are given; more significantly they are given to be repeated. They interconnect with the exigency that architecture must function. As architecture becomes sculpture, for example, it ceases to be architecture. While the limit condition may define the architectural at its most emphatic, it

remains the case that architecture will always have to hold itself apart from other generic possibilities.

Continuing the analogy with poetry means having to allow for the possibility that there will be an analog within architecture for that state of affairs in which within poetry there is the continual movement between *connu* and *inconnu*. One does not negate the other. More important, within poetry the insistence of *inconnu*—and within the *in* of *inconnu* it is vital to hear the work of a productive negativity—works to hold the form of the already given in place. It is at this stage that a more detailed argument in regard to the role of *l'informe* becomes necessary. Here, it can only be sketched in outline form.

Working with the necessity that architecture must function, questions then will only ever concern the formal presence of that function. However, there cannot be a mere formalism since the nature of the function is already determined in advance. There is already a conception of the domestic, the pedagogic, for example, that is given by the work of tradition. Innovation can take place, but only to the extent that it

holds the particular determination of the specific function in place. Countering the working of tradition demands that which will undo the specificity of the form/function relation. In other words, rather than either the nihilism of destruction or a didactic architecture that prescribes other possibilities, there will be an architecture that in sustaining the specificity of function allows that function to be transformed in the process. The transformation, however, needs to be thought outside the work of teleology. In other words, it needs to open up the question of the domestic, the pedagogic, public space versus private, for example, and it will always be necessary to insist that there are only examples; while holding and allowing for the reiteration of function. What architecture will sustain is an opening in which the nature of function is being explored, investigated and questioned, while still allowing for function. In temporal terms, even though the building is built, despite the fact that it is complete, it remains, at the time, incomplete. Given that the incomplete will work with the complete, since both occur simultaneously, what this entails is the copresence of a material condition—the complete—that is

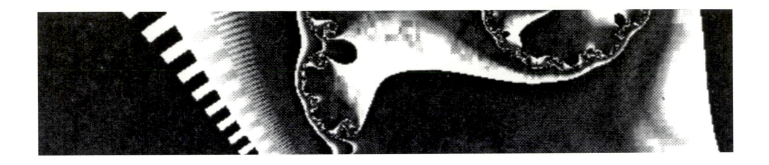

always working with that which is immaterially present, namely the continual condition and conditioning of the incomplete. They will be present in their difference, generating a complex architecture. Complexity in architecture therefore will be a consequence of the work of *l'informe*. Here it is necessary to leave aside a more detailed analysis of *l'informe*.

The demanding problem, the problem in which it becomes possible to situate the architectural, will concern the way program comes to be related to the generation of form. What emerged from Bataille was a way of thinking through the exigency that relates form to architecture—even though that exigency was linked to poetry—while relegating to the symbolic or the monumental the question of program or function. What this meant is that architecture was thought outside the hold of an ontology of movement and self-effectuation. Bataille was unable to link architecture to the question of form. A significant part of the reason for this setup is the equation, on Bataille's part, of architecture and building. As such, architecture was always understood as a fait accompli, an object whose work was already

accomplished. Indeed, a direct result of this situation is that architecture and form were necessarily distanced. While not dealing ostensibly with architecture, the architectural imperative within Deleuze's work is linked to the production of form. However, here the response to Deleuze cannot just be that programmatic concerns came to be left out and that therefore this imperative is badly formulated and in need of the resuscitating addition. The response must be that the way in which form is produced precludes a consideration of program precisely because of the way in which difference—in this instance articulated in terms of the opposition between the homogeneous and the heterogeneous—and thus ontology figure within his undertaking. It is this movement that must be traced.

Rather that try to offer a synoptic reading here, emphasis will be placed on the way in which a distinction between smooth and striated space is established in *A Thousand Plateaus*. As a preliminary caveat, it should be noted that in this work Deleuze is not writing about architecture. His direct discussion of the architectural occurs in *The Fold*.

What makes Baroque architecture of particular interest is that it is defined by a scission between facade and inside, on the one hand, and exterior and interior on the other. What this means is that with this form of architecture in place of the determining hold of the opposition between surface and depth, there is a rearticulation of the Baroque emblem of "fold following fold" and thus a "unity in complication." Leibniz's insight, for Deleuze, is that distinction and thus difference allows for cohesion. Descartes failed to grasp this philosophical point. In Deleuze's terms,

> It is undoubtedly Descartes' mistake ... to have thought that the real distinction between parts entailed separability.[5]

The point at issue in this instance is not the distinction between Leibniz and Descartes. Central to what is at stake here is, first, the nature of the relationship between parts and whole and therefore, in the second place, the conception of difference, unity in difference, that informs the already identified distinction between parts and wholes. The copresence of distinction and inseparability becomes a way of introducing the nature of the

distinction between smooth and striated space.

The Cartesian "mistake" identified by Deleuze refers to the necessity, for Descartes, of establishing distinctions between given points, axioms, parts of a whole, by an act of reduction. Not only were complexes generated by an amalgam of simples, all of which exist at the same time, the simples could be separated and thus that which generated the complex could be identified. What enabled this move to take place was that there was a unity and singularity that could be attributed to the "thing." It is, of course, this particular position that is most clearly articulated by Descartes in the *Second Set of Replies to the Meditations,* in which he argues that the "idea" of the sun is the sun "existing" in the understanding. The "idea" and the "thing" are not identical. It is rather that the Cartesian "idea" is coextensive with that of which it is the idea. This coextensivity brings with it inevitable ontological considerations. Moreover, it is only by having recourse to ontology that it becomes possible to think the difference between Descartes and Leibniz. The counter to Descartes, the other ontological possibility, can

be found in Leibniz's formulation of the necessarily limited nature of perception in *Monadology.*

In *Monadology* Leibniz explains how there can be a move from one perception to another.

> The activity of the internal principle which produces change from one perception to another may be called Appetition. It is true that desire *[l'appétit]* cannot always fully attain to the whole perception to which it aims, but it always attains some of it and attains to new perceptions.[6]

What is identified here as the "internal principle" is process or movement. It is the continuity of desire. The continuity of desiring—here understood as a state of affairs that is necessarily ontological in nature—is not incompatible with the presentation of different forms, different modes of presentation—in other words, different perceptions. Here the site of multiplicity is not located in a multitude of different entities taken together—as will be suggested, this is the Cartesian conception of complexity—but rather multiplicity exists to the extent that it is located in unity. Perception is part of the existence of this form of multiplicity. Moving

from one state to the next, from one presentation to the next, is explicable only in terms of process; more exactly, it is explicable only in terms of an ontology of becoming.

Locating multiplicity in unity presents a problem for any interpretation of Leibniz. There are two elements within this formulation. In other words, there are two sites at which it becomes possible to locate multiplicity in unity. The first involves recognizing difference between perceptions. Each perception is incomplete in relation to the demand of appetition, and yet each perception is proper to the monad, Hence, there is multiplicity in unity. The second is the more demanding. It involves distinguishing between "desire" or appetition, on the one hand, and perception, on the other. The monad becomes the divide between these two moments. In a letter to de Bosses, Leibniz defines the monad's substance as "force" *(vis).* Force is ontologically similar to desire or appetition. Both entail movement resisting representation. Perception, on the other hand, amounts to the way in which at any point in time the monad is able to be represented. This is the monad's appearance. Perception is necessarily connected to

representation and to that extent, ontologically, bears no similarity to the ontology of desire and force. In this latter case the question of multiplicity in unity has become complex.

The first instance provides a conception of multiplicity in which in the one there is the continuity of the folded multiplicity. This is what Leibniz meant by the soul's infinite folds or the labyrinthine coils of matter bringing another domain of the infinite into play. Here, the question of what distinguishes one perception from another, or one fold from the opening of another is that which is given by what Deleuze identifies in another context as "a process of continuous variation." It will be precisely this conception of multiplicity that is at work in Deleuze's description of movement. However, it is the second sense of multiplicity that gives rise to a conception of difference, and thus to the heterogeneous as marked by the presence of an insistent and anoriginal irreducibility. Indeed it will be an irreducibility at the origin that will stand in sharp contradistinction to variety and diversity. It will be this demanding divide within Leibniz—a demand

engendering two fundamentally different conceptions of multiplicity—that will need to inform the analysis of the distinction between smooth and striated space.

This twofold possibility for space does not simply have an important philosophical dimension; it has also played a fundamental role in architectural strategies whose primary concern have been the generation of form. Not only does the architectural element endure, Deleuze also alludes to the already present urban dimension occurring with this distinction. While the city may be striated space, there is a smoothing of the city occurring in part through the "activity of city dwellers who have no need of striation." The real force of the distinction lies in there being two different spatial qualities, such that by virtue of this difference there are ways in which connections can either be staged or realized. A start can be made with what is described in *A Thousand Plateaus* as as the "technological model."[7] Here striation becomes linked to the incorporation of the defining presence of the vertical and the horizontal. In the case of a fabric, the only intrusion on the infinite is additive in nature. The infinite is

not internal but occurs because a "fabric can be infinite in length." It is in contrast to this conception of the technological that felt emerges as the "anti-fabric." It will be in terms of felt and patchwork that it becomes possible to identify some of the defining characteristics of smooth space and, more important in this case, to note the particular conception of repetition that is at work within it.

Felt is described in the following terms:

> An aggregate of intrication of this kind is in no way homogeneous: it is nevertheless smooth ... it is in principle infinite, open and unlimited in every direction; it has neither top nor bottom nor center; it does not assign fixed and mobile elements but rather distributes a continuous variation. (pp. 475–76)

Patchwork is assigned similar qualities. Again the important motif

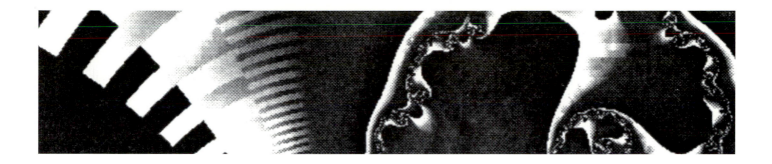

is the relationship between repetition and a potential infinite. In is in these terms that patchwork is defined as an

> amorphous collection of juxtaposed pieces that can be joined together in an infinite number of ways. (p. 476)

In working through these examples, it is essential to retain the fact that central to this undertaking is the problem of the generation of form and with it the generation of the activity of spacing.

Both felt and patchwork admit of a certain heterogeneity. It is this conception of the heterogeneous that can be understood as the consequence of repetition. Homogeneity is excluded precisely because of the "continuous variation." (It will emerge that it is this formulation which will come to define the relationship between the haptic and the smooth.) While these descriptions relate to material, they can be taken as yielding a certain architectural practice. However, the question here concerns not the practice per se but two interrelated theoretical issues. The first concerns repetition; the precise conception

of repetition at work within what Deleuze calls "continuous variety." The second relates to the heterogeneous. What conception of heterogeneity stems from "variety"? In this context specifically, how is the heterogeneity of felt to be understood? It is with these questions that it will be possible to conclude.

The way of answering these questions stems as much from Leibniz as from Bataille. Leibniz's conception of multiplicity in unity allowed for the possibility of a founding complexity. Complexity was ontological in nature. Unity was the copresence of two ontologically distinct and hence irreducible elements. In the case of Bataille, what emerged was the productive interplay of form and *l'informe.* Rather than generating a mere formalism, these two elements provide the possibility of maintaining within a unity what has been identified thus far as a productive negativity. It will be in terms of this form of negativity that it will be possible for architecture to enter into a transformative engagement with function while eschewing the retention of the didactic and the prescriptive. It is in terms of the presence of the

incomplete, copresent with the already complete building, that it becomes possible to allow for a transformation on the level of function. Transformation presupposes the inscribed presence of a function to be transformed. What this means is that criticality, once freed from the hold of either a utopian promise or a teleological prescription, is linked to maintaining a fragile opening that will be the work's work. What will enable that work to unfold is the impossibility of reducing the material to the immaterial. Criticality therefore depends upon a conception of heterogeneity that is marked by an ontological irreducibility.

Leibniz held the key. And yet this was not the Leibniz utilized by Deleuze. The Deleuzian conception of multiplicity ends up being governed by a unity that is there at the origin, what he described in *Différence et Répétition* in the proposition "Being is univocal."[8] This becomes clear in the examples of both patchwork and felt. While there are internal differences, felt reams the continuity of the same material. Difference understood as variety is based on the retention of a founding unity. Patchwork offers a similar setup. While one material

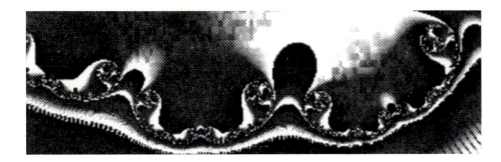

may differ from another—wool as opposed to silk, cotton rather than linen—and while designs may differ—plain rather than striped, floral as opposed to paisley; it remains the case that what is at work within all of these is the repetition of material. All are types of cloth. None is different outside the realm of appearance. Repetition here, therefore, is governed by the Same. Heterogeneity cannot escape the hold of unity as it is a repetition of the Same. The patches are not identical, but they are all the same. In more general terms, therefore, it is unclear to what extent the term heterogeneity is actually appropriate to describe this setup.

What this means architecturally is that a design process which can only engage with a repetition that is structured by the Same and with multiplicity, and hence a conception of complexity that amounts to a diversity that has unity as its ground, becomes unidimensional, not formally but in terms of providing the possibility for a critical architecture. Formal innovations taken as ends in themselves cannot introduce the critical since they do not retain the ground of the critical itself. The critical is contingent on the retention of a strong

relationship between form and function. Thinking that retention, however, necessitates articulating it within the productive yet irreducible presence of the material and the immaterial.

Notes

1. The following text is the basis of my lecture given at the conference "Emerging Complexities," held at Columbia University's GSAP. The lecture forms a companion piece to my "Building Philosophy: Towards Architectural Theory" (*AA Files*, no. 37, July 1997). The work of Bataille, Derrida and Deleuze that figures in both has been reworked in order to develop a conception of architectural theory whose force is derived in part from Bataille's conception of *l'informe* and in part from what I have called an ontology of "anoriginal heterogeneity" in *The Plural Event* (London: Routledge, 1993). This work will appear in my forthcoming book *Complex Spacing: Relating Philosophy and Architecture* (Routledge, 1998).

2. All references to Georges Bataille are to *Oeuvres complètes* (Paris: Gallimard, 1970). The references are given in the text; first volume, then page number. All translations are my own.

3. The central text by Maurice Blanchot discussed here is *La bête de Lascaux* (Montpellier: Fata Morgana, 1982). I have discussed this text and the question of a productive negativity in much greater detail in "Figuring Self-Identity: Blanchot's Bataille," in J. Steyn, ed., *Other than Identity, The Subject, Politics and Aesthetics* (Manchester: Manchester University Press, 1996).

4. A more extensive treatment of *l'informe* can be found in *Complex Spacing*. I have left the term in French, as the translation of *l'informe* — "formless"— fails to confront the problem of how to interpret the nature of the negative. How is the prefix *in* to be understood? Moveover, "formless" leaves aside the productive nature of what is designated by this term. In fact in emphasizing whatever representational qualities *l'informe* may have, the English translation does so at the expense of any productive or economic force inherent in the concept.

5. Gilles Deleuze. *The Fold: Leibniz and the Baroque*. Tom Conley, trans. (Minneapolis: University of Minnesota Press, 1993), 68.

6. Gottfried Wilhelm Leibniz. *The Mondology*. R. Latta, ed. and trans. (Oxford: Oxford University Press, 1948). I have attempted a more sustained reading of Leibniz that follows this direction in *The Plural Event*. (London: Routlege, 1993), 112–29.

7. Gilles Deleuze. *A Thousand Plateaus*. Brian Massumi, trans. (Minneapolis: University of Minnesota Press, 1987). All page numbers are given in the text.

8. Gilles Deleuze. *Différence et Répétition* (Paris: PUF, 1996), 52. Since writing this lecture I have become aware that Alain Badiou's recent book on Deleuze, *Deleuze: "La clameur de l'Etre"* (Paris: Hachette, 1997) advances a more sustained version of the argument sketched here. I hope to engage with Badiou's treatment in *Complex Spacing*.

THE ENEMY OF ARCHITECTURE

Sometimes I feel that architecture is my enemy. Rather than architecture, the body is my concern. Thoughts associated with artistic expressions linked intimately to the body have been my focus. Painting and sculpture, poetry and prose, dance and theater, even cinema all have relations to the body in various modes of disjunction and connection. The relations are not unique, and there is not simply one body. Each thought or expression intervenes in different aspects of the body, transforms it and creates a new type of body. Style in art is inseparable from the body. In Japanese, the word that corresponds to literary style *(buntai)* means "body of phrases" and is used for all the arts. Style is the body of art and is linked to the organic aspects of art. Works of art are not separable from idea and form; they are concerned with the body. They create it and then problematize it. The fact that the art of the twentieth century has constructed a newer intimate relation with the body, compared to classical or nineteenth-century art, is very important.

But the body is not an object that is obvious or known in advance. Gilles Deleuze and Felix Guattari discovered in Antonin Artaud's texts the concept of the "body without organs" and applied it to an analysis of capitalism. The body without organs is related to all the paradoxical and schizophrenic aspects of capitalism—all of its tendencies to violate and transgress centers, borders and territories. At the same time it indicates a very special state of the body, problematizing the traditional image of the body in Western metaphysics as a dichotomy of mind and body.

Architecture is opposed to the body, insofar as it is immobile, grounded in the earth, endowed with the forms and structures of it, inseparable from sedentary life, linked intimately with state, capitalism and industry and more or less authoritarian. Architecture is inorganic. It neither breathes nor vibrates, possessing little that is delicate, flexible or unstable. Constructed according to strict plan, it has no opaque and haphazard aspects, compared with painting or sculpture. Rather than an endless, solitary experience, it is a collective work determined by structure, capital and the duration

of its construction. Its structure is determined primarily by a symmetrical regularity, coherent unities and geometric homogeneity.

Perhaps it is true that architecture already has a history of very sophisticated thinking in regard to the question of the body, or bio-organic elements. I pretend to ignore it. Certainly architecture is a container that envelops human bodies, a machine that determines the distribution, the encounter, the movement and the connection of human bodies. The body itself is a kind of machine reproducing, consuming and exhausting itself until death, connected and disconnected with other bodies. What Deleuze and Guattari insisted on in *Anti-Oedipus* —considering the body as a machine—was this aspect of open connection and process of production among human and animal bodies. The baby's mouth actualizes in a coupling with the mother's nipples—a machine. The infant's gender, excrement and food compose another machine along with his/her mother's and father's bodies. Moreover, these machines receive all kinds of effects and forces, whether social, historical or political, which penetrate the

bodies of familial members, and all these machines are traversed by forces of nature and the universe. Architecture may also be a machine among all these machines, open to other connections, forming all sorts of machines with human bodies.

Indeed the books of Deleuze and Guattari are full of rich concepts concerning architecture, technology, space and urbanism. Opposed to centering, hierarchy, homogeneity, symmetry and the tracing of the identical—all these things they call *arborescent schema*—is the concept of the rhizome, which proposes another organization defined as decentralized, anti-hierarchical, heterogeneous and dissymmetrical. The rhizome is neither merely chaos nor disorder, although it sometimes looks like catastrophic chaos. The chapters of Deleuze's *A Thousand Plateaus* are all attempts to discover and elaborate models of this other order that is not a disorder (such as the molecular, the smooth, body without organs, micropolitics). In a sense, the whole of Deleuzian philosophy is an attempt to analyze, define and create this other order.

Architecture is inseparable from the question of how to occupy, cut and connect spaces, how to carve, transform and distribute materials. Architecture determines human perception, body, action, gesture and relations. It is universal and determinative in human life. Guattari rather than Deleuze tried to intervene in questions of architecture and urbanism, offering visions of architecture capable of producing alternative desire—other connections of desire, that is to say, aesthetic and social mutations that oppose the uniform and functional aspects of modern architecture and urbanism, which tend to separate, control and constrict human relations.

Although, on the one hand, architecture imprisons the activity of *design* (decorating powers, capitals and ruling classes) on the other hand, architecture reflects a very complex, immanent, impersonal network of forces characterizing a new type of power that functions like a rhizome. Contemporary power is a set of functions that can no longer be attributed to any personality, any political party, any class, although we can never underestimate the visible forces such as the mass media, multinational companies and so on. Earlier I opposed architecture to the body. I can no longer maintain this position: the body, as well as architecture, is integrated into open connections of machines and into complex networks of invisible powers.

The "body without organs" is a phrase that appears quite often in the dramatist and poet Antonin Artaud's texts, particularly those written during his last years. Before exhibiting intense schizophrenic symptoms in the 1930s, the young Artaud suffered from a catalepsy of the body and a paralysis of thinking. He described this metamorphosis of body and thought very precisely, calling it a "nothingness that does not possess organs."

At the time of this crisis he adopted an excessive faith in the body, asserting that he believed in nothing but that which touches the body, though strangely enough, he was radically opposed to the organs. Why is Artaud so hostile to organs? For him, the organs are only functions, articulations, divisions and determinations forced on the body. Of course the mind is also based on the same kinds of determinations. Thus Artaud refuses all limitations deriving from the mind but adhered to those associated with the body, insofar as the organs were excluded.

The human body is never simply biological. It is trained, managed, determined and made up of social, political and historical assemblages. Morality, medicine—health care of all kinds—do not merely nurse the body; they are devices that produce the body. The last work of Michel Foucault addresses the kind of historical mechanism that penetrates the body.

Claiming the body, Artaud denies the organs. This ambivalent position expresses Artaud's resistance to the Western system of separation, determination and incarceration imposed on the body. Such a system penetrates not only into the mind but also into the body, dividing mind and body, while drawing a parallel between the two. As an avant-garde revolutionary artist, Artaud conceived a revolution of the body, or by the body, different from the Marxist revolution of infrastructure and the surrealist revolution of aesthetics and the unconscious, to which he was committed for a time.

Artaud wrote an essay entitled "The Theater and the Past," in which he argues that we cannot attribute the past to an organic process that attacks organs. Instead, he proposes another vision of the body, one that overcomes determination and closure through the medium of the organs. His theater was just such an experience of this other body.

The West has not simply repressed the body. On the contrary, the ancient Greeks admired the beauty of a well-trained body, and Christian icons focused on the naked Jesus, transforming it. Perhaps no other civilization is as interested and fascinated with the image of the body as that of the West. Thus the body is represented, idolized and imaged. At the same time the existence of the body and all the differences and singularities that establish the reality of the body are excluded. In order to avoid turning the body into an icon, we need to invent another mode of living with the body. Certainly with the idea of the body without organs Artaud conceived a singular revolution in the reality of the body. And in his final days, the violence of his hospitalization caused him to politicize the whole history concerning the exclusion of the body. His writings during this period form a kind of apocalypse of bodies.

The mind, or consciousness, is firmly determined by historical and political continuity and is closely linked to the field of powers in this context. The fact that psychoanalysis discovered the unconscious is important insofar as this shift to egocentric tendencies of thought. But to be confronted with the body raises another question that is no less important. In thinking about the body, Artaud was obliged to think as well about restrictions imposed on the body. It has become impossible for art and philosophy to ignore this paradox.

A short passage from Artaud's text about the Belgian writer Maurice Maeterlink concerns architecture: "The Philosophy of Maeterlinck is like a temple in action. Each stone draws an image. It does not constitute on any account a system. It has neither architecture nor form. It has volume, a height, a density." Volume, height and density without architecture or form characterize the body without organs, in which Artaud suffers through his extraordinary thought and grueling experiences.

This body is not merely organic but also inorganic, given its state as a machine. Many have remarked that the arrival of the steam engine led to significant change in the

image of the body, bringing about notions like energy, production and consumption. The human body then entered into an unknown dimension that tended toward the inorganic. Even the living and the organic, presumed to be given by God and therefore untouchable, became manipulable. The border that separates the organic and the inorganic became increasingly blurred. Artaud detected the signs and the threats of all these changes through the idea and the reality of the body without organs.

I will now proceed to change my viewpoint somewhat. Jacques Lacan remarked that something new happened between the age of Hegel and the age of Freud: this something was the arrival of the machine, and the body as machine. A different notion of time appeared with it. For example in Bergson's theory, time is a pure object for thought. Hegel's dialectic was essentially a way to idealize time as history, which would bring about the telos of his famous "absolute spirit." Modern philosophy or thought is based on a new concept of time. But whether or not it is idealized, time is inextricable from the idea of continuity and totality. This is true not only for Bergson, who thought about time as duration

and memory that are neither divisible nor representable in the mode of extension, but also for Freud, who conceptualized the human being on the basis of his/her childhood, which was determined by the parental relationship. In both cases time was crucial, spurring on a new form of synthesis and continuity for uncertain humans in time.

Time is neither visible nor divisible, although in general, space is visible and divisible. It is this invisibility of time that sometimes produces mysterious, unifying and fascinating ideas even in the most modern thinkers of time. In this sense, the contribution of philosophy and psychoanalysis is not without ambiguity.

I think of Michel Foucault as someone who suddenly discovered architecture in philosophy. As is well known, in *Discipline and Punish* Foucault focused on Jeremy Bentham's Panopticon—a system of observing prisoners from a circumference located at a distance from the center whereby the observers were invisible to the prisoners, and therefore could be present or not. For Foucault this architecture of the prison was what determined the system of power

that has spanned the entirety of modern Western civilization. Instead of speaking of social structures that accumulate and unify history, evolution and memory, Foucault focused his analysis merely on a spatial operation that actualizes a mutation that cuts across society. Whether visible or invisible, this architecture is not so pleasant for those who live in it, are enclosed in it and are permanently observed by it. In this system the human body is determined, incarcerated and occasionally provoked or stimulated to desire, passion and action. Such architecture causes discontinuity and ruptures in the unifying concept of history and time, determining and producing series of mutated spaces. The question might be: Is there another mode of architecture that could open, liberate and recreate human relationships in contrast to the Panopticon?

What is at stake is the idea of an invisible body and architecture and the invisible connections between the two. Architecture may be a part of a giant, open infinite body without organs.

The Japanese architect Arata Isozaki wrote a text entitled

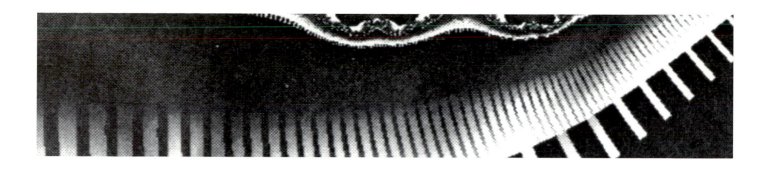

Invisible City in 1967. Flying low over Tokyo and looking down on this city in which center and outskirts are contiguous, he compared it to Jackson Pollock's canvases covered by a chaos of drippings. He also referred to Los Angeles viewed from the sky as a "mobile city" composed mostly of caravans, capable of appearing and disappearing in one night, having no form or outline and lacking any physical or visible appearance. On these landscapes he superimposed his memory of Tokyo as it appeared bombed and reduced to rubble in World War II. We can imagine a correspondence of these visions of the city to the notion of an invisible architecture.

What is perplexing is that this invisible city is also integrated within all the functions of power belonging to high-tech capitalism; it expresses one aspect of this power. Although it appears to indicate an anarchic and free proliferation, mobility and rhizome, all these flows or lines of flight can play a role in protecting power from gaps and tears in its borders. In this sense, contemporary power possesses no center but only borders; it functions continually on the borders that exist everywhere.

Earlier on I opposed architecture to the body because of the body's mobility, opacity, organicity, uncertainty—all differences and nuances that the body envelops. But the body as well as architecture is determined and structured by society and history—a machine imbricated with various forces, materialities and institutions. Artaud attempted to extract and purify the body from these intruders. We do not know if he succeeded.

The body is both in space and time. It can share the unifying function of time as well as the connections and disconnections of space. Architecture is situated in the whole range of variation that extend from the visible to the invisible. There is an architecture that is disembodied and imprisons life, but there is also the possibility of an architecture that traverses, cracks and breaks this disembodied imprisoning architecture.

PETER EISENMAN
CRITICAL ARCHITECTURE IN A GEOPOLITICAL WORLD

Eisenman Architects: Urban competition for the Kingelhöfer Triangle, Berlin, 1995. Computer rendering.

According to most political analysts, a new condition of ideological politics exists today, one that no longer addresses the class struggle of communism versus capitalism, of First World versus Third World: that condition is geopolitics. Geopolitics, despite the increasing mediation of the globe as a single entity, seems to involve the notion of location as a political factor. The "geo," in this sense, stands for geography, as opposed to geology. Involved in the geopolitical condition is the idea that since Western politics finds itself unable to continue to provide for the economic, social and political infrastructure that it imposed on such areas as the Middle East in the nineteenth century, the emerging Pacific Rim and Muslim countries, in their particular geopolitical locations, are no longer necessarily dependent on the Western world for their politics. Capital, particularly,

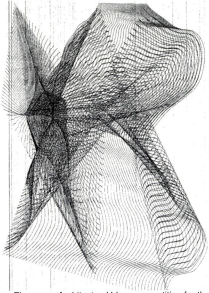

Eisenman Architects: Urban competition for the Kingelhöfer Triangle, Berlin, 1995. Site diagram.

international capital, has replaced ideological politics as political currency. If there is in fact an ideological politics today, it can be seen as an idea of global capital, which has replaced the class struggle as an ideological content.

These are two very different views of reality, and as we know, reality is a concept that is also ideological. According to a continuous view of history, the idea of Western capital evolved over 200 years. It grew out of a view of history—again, ideological—as the revolutionary and ideological politics of a class struggle against the "*ancien régime.*" Most manifestations of Western colonialism were grounded in this ideology. Today, when colonialism as politics, is no longer seen as a dominant ideology, politics is replaced by the notion of capital, and, more specifically, the capital of

location. This is the difference between the ideological politics grounded in the nineteenth century and the notion of location as a problem of capital in the late twentieth century. It is possible to assume that the major banking centers in the world fifty years from now will be Hong Kong, Shanghai, Kuala Lumpur, Jakarta and Singapore, because of their location. Within the economics, as opposed to the politics of place, what role does architecture play, since architecture is assumed to be grounded in place? But first one must ask the question, what role did architecture play in the ideological politics of the last 200 years?

All movements of the avant-garde, beginning in the late eighteenth century and extending to about 1933, were related to the development of ideological politics. The first model for this is Piranesi's work on the

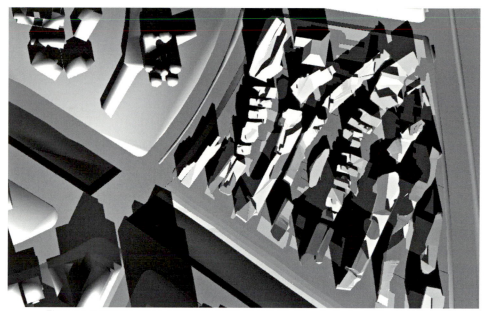

Site diagram iteration.

Eisenman Architects: Urban competition for the Kingelhöfer Triangle, Berlin, 1995. Computer rendering.

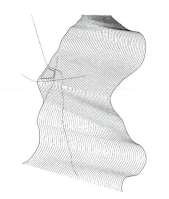

Site diagram iteration.

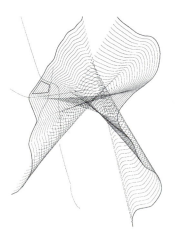

Site diagram iteration.

Campo Marzio. It corresponds in time roughly to the development of the notion of an ideological politics, working against what would be called the "*ancien régime.*" Until this time, there was no architecture related to ideological politics because ideological politics since before the French Revolution, the notion of architecture and class had not been at issue. Even the shift from so-called theocentric politics to an anthropocentric politics, which witnessed the movement from the Gothic to the Renaissance to the Baroque, never took into account the question of class.

In this context, it is important to note that Manfredo Tafuri calls Piranesi the first critical architect. He notes that for the first time in Piranesi, the negative is introduced into the discourse of architecture as a problematic. Whether or not one agrees with Tafuri, one of the aspects of a critical architecture is the incorporation of an alternative view of reality into architecture. In this context, Immanuel Kant's formulation is important. He spoke of the critical as that condition of knowledge which speaks of the possibility in knowledge of knowledge. The idea of the possible is different than the idea of the negative. It is not enough to have architecture represent a certain condition of political thought, rather, if one substitutes being for knowledge, then criticality is the possibility of being in being. For architecture to be critical it would be something more than an iconic or functional representation, rather it would be the possibility of architecture to manifest its own being.

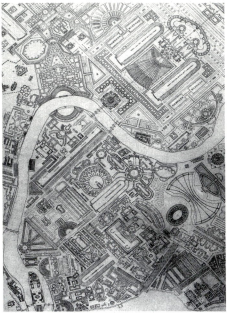
(fig. 1) Pianesi, Nolli Map of Rome, 1754.

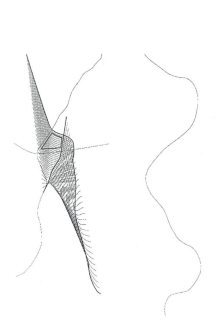

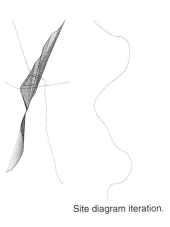
Site diagram iteration.

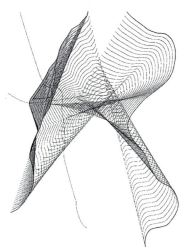
Site diagram iteration.

(fig. 2) Piranesi: Campo Marzio, 1762.

Site diagram iteration.

Site diagram iteration.

Two images (figs.1and 2), both drawings by Piranesi, can be used to illustrate this point. Figure one is taken from the Nolli Map of 1754. It is Piranesi who drew the first Nolli Map. It was Piranesi who first thought to depict the public spaces, both the exterior public spaces and the interior public spaces, as void with the other interior spaces rendered in black poche. This is a condition of what has come to be known as the figure-ground drawing, in which the objects in the city seem to be cut out, as it were, of a black ground and become white figures. The Piazza Navona, the churches and other public figural elements are deployed in a relationship of figure to ground. In 1762 Piranesi began to draw an area of Imperial Rome called the Campo Marzio. This is an entirely different relationship of figure to ground, and thus speaks, for the first time, of another kind of

urbanism. It can be called a figure-figure urbanism, where the figures are ungrounded. The issue of the ungrounded or the unframed figure, or the figure that is no longer dialectically conceived as being on a ground, is important. In Piranesi's drawing of Hadrian's villa, for example, there is a collision of figures, seen in relationship to a ground. In the Campo Marzio drawing, the ground is as if a light behind a figure of figures. The space between the figures which is usually understood as a ground, is filled up with further figures, which can be called interstitial figures. Axes in the Campo Marzio are always marked by figures, and when two figures collide they are not mediated by ground but rather by interstitial figures.

110

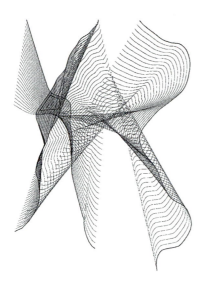

Site diagram iteration.

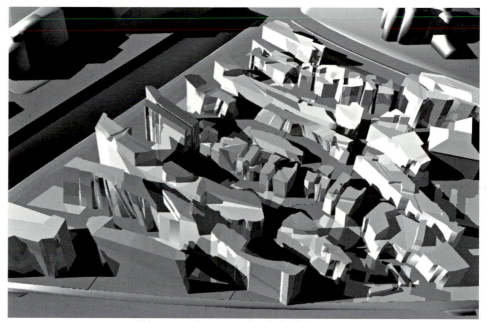

Urban competition for the Kingelhöfer Triangle, Berlin, 1995. Computer rendering.

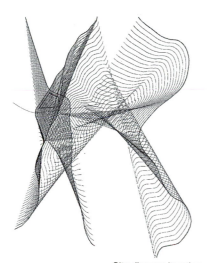

Site diagram iteration.

Piranesi's plan is critical in several ways. First, because there is the possibility of another kind of knowledge being portrayed in architecture. The possibility that architecture could be seen as ungrounded—not only ungrounded in a figure-ground relationship, but also ungrounded in relation to its linguistic and historical traditions. This idea of criticality is different from Henri Lefebvre's categories of historical space and abstract space. Lefebvre asserts that the historical is a natural phenomenon, whereas abstract space is a code imposed on a message. His view is that historical space starts from messages that then evolve into codes, while abstract space starts with codes and devolves into messages. What Lefebvre is talking about is a notion that space is a ground, and he assumes that all space is grounded. According to

Lefebvre, a code, necessarily, involves abstraction. My suggestion is that Piranesi's Campo Marzio is no more an abstraction than is the Nolli plan. It speaks of a different kind of space, not an historical space nor an abstract space, but one that could be called a critical space. Such an idea does not abstract space out of history, but rather space is projected back into the history of the discourse itself.

The French philosopher Gilles Deleuze has another way of describing this condition, which is useful for understanding Piranesi. Deleuze suggests that there are two views of any kind of discourse. One is an extensive view. For example, Kant's view of space-time as a series of discrete relational entities, as a series that follows one from the other, can be seen as an extensive view. Most conditions of

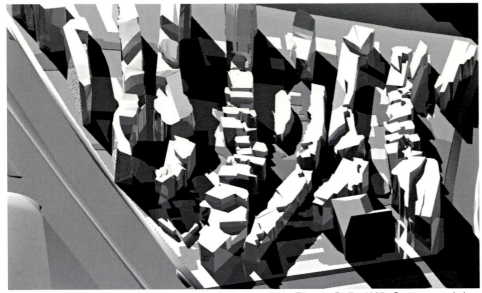

Urban competition for the Kingelhöfer Triangle, Berlin, 1995. Computer rendering.

TEBAULICHER WETTBEWERB KLINGELHÖFER-DREIECK SÜD   1
ZEPTIONELLES SCHEMA

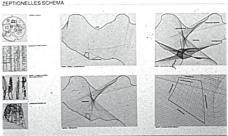

Competition panel.

architectural thought are based in this view. The extensive view continues today precisely because there has been no examination of the other view of the way space and time might be configured. Rather, such an extensive view has been normalized in such a way that figure and ground constitute the dialogue of urban space and that the ground is always the space rather than the figure—that the ground always precedes the figure and that the figure is always grounded. They are grounded in both an extensive view of history but also in our desire for such a conception of ground.

A second or intensive view of architecture's history assumes a conceptual internality for architecture that is repressed by the normalization of the extensive. In Piranesi, space and time no longer necessarily defined as figure and ground, but are rather defined by some other ungrounded intensive view of the world. In this view, Piranesi's drawing of Campo Marzio could be seen as an intensive view into an interiority of architecture that was previously hidden is one of many possibilities of detaching architecture from its previous modes of legitimation.

In this context, can be seen as a continuum that subsumes the notion of international capital in an extensive view of history. Both ideological politics and international capitalism require a certain figure-ground continuum. Every major proposal after Piranesi—be it Haussmann's plan for Paris, Sitte's plan for Vienna, Le Corbusier's plans for the Ville Radieuse or the Plan Voisin—deal with a similar notion of figure and ground. They assume that this is the way urban ideas are

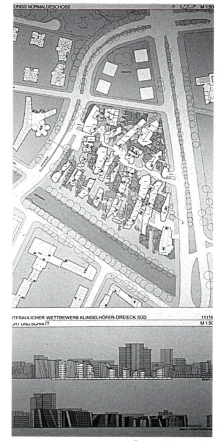

Competition panel.

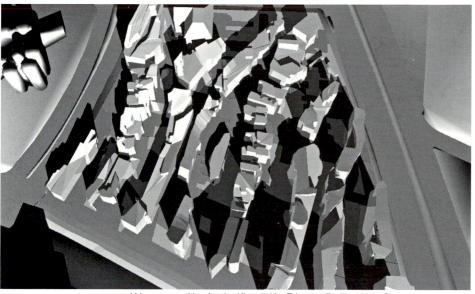

Urban competition for the Kingelhöfer Triangle, Berlin, 1995. Computer rendering.

formulated. The only modern plans that do not use figure and ground are Hilbersheimer's Siedlung plans for Berlin and Chicago. These have been severely criticized by such urbanists as Leon Krier and Colin Rowe because they lack any figural relationships: they have no facades, or fronts and backs of buildings. The idea of a figure-ground relationship is assumed to be a natural condition that is an historical message, rather than a convention or a code. In fact, both the Nolli drawing and the Campo Marzio drawing by Piranesi are codes. One is no more grounded in the idea of history than the other; they are both inventions of a way of describing reality. As such, they should be seen for what they are, that is, equivalent kinds of instruments. One is no better than the other; each merely provides a different possibility for looking at architecture.

The continuity of a figure-ground discourse today leaves the idea of the possibility of "being" in knowledge, the original Kantian proposition, unanswered because it assumes says that the language or internality of architecture is both stable and known.

The reason one drawing is assumed to be natural and the other to be a code or a convention, is because architects unwittingly assume an extensive view of their own discourse. They assume the continuity of history like the continuity of a space-time framing proposed by Kant and Hegel. This leaves unexamined alternative propositions for an idea of space-time. The idea of an ungrounded depth for an architectural discourse, and the idea of a figure-figure urbanism is both a critique of Kant's aesthetics and the aesthetic formulations of the Nolli plan.

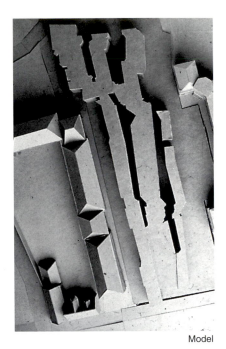

Eisenman Architects: Contemprary Arts Center and Regional National Music Conservatory competition. Tours, France, 1994. Model.

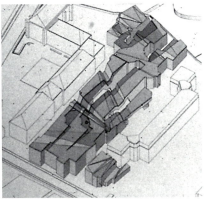

Rendering.

Any idea of architecture's interiority assumes architecture to be a three-dimensional space that shelters or encloses. This view acknowledges that architecture deals with the forming of function. While architecture will inevitably deal with some forming of function, this notion of forming is no longer needed to legitimize an architecture. The concept of the space of architecture—that architecture is always the relationship between an interior and an exterior, between a sacred and a profane; that architecture shelters, encloses, defines, places, locates; that cities must have places—derives from two ideas. First, from the idea that architecture is a grounding; and second, from the idea that architecture reflects a desire for grounding and that the locus of that desire is projected onto architecture. Therefore, it is assumed that figure-ground as place making is merely, the projection of this desire onto architecture. It is possible to loosen that desire from the notion of placing, forming, enclosing, and sheltering necessary to architecture in order to see and understand a different kind of architectural condition.

Walter Benjamin said that most people view architecture in a state of distraction. They do not look at architecture as they view sculpture, in other words, as a moment in time of reflection. They do not listen to music in the way they look at architecture; they do not read books in this way. In other words, architecture is basically unframed. Architecture is without a framing notion because of the assumption of the desire for architecture to be grounded, to be located. Since architecture responds quite readily to that desire, it can be treated

Model.

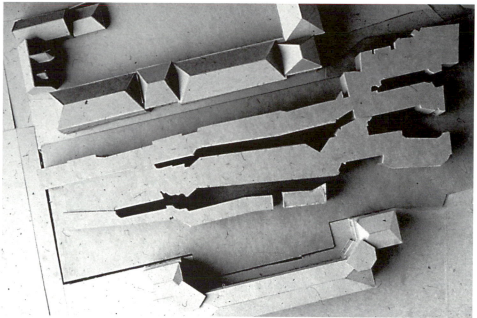

Eisenman Architects: Contemprary Arts Center and Regional National Music Conservatory competition. Tours, France, 1994. Model.

Sections.

distractedly. But again if that desire could be displaced, it might create the conditions for an undistracted architecture.

In the age of information, capital is no longer willing to invest in anything other than what it considers a necessary infrastructure. It no longer sees architecture as anything other than the functional necessity of capital infrastructure. It no longer sees in architecture any symbolic value, because architecture in this context is seen as something casual. Media, in the age of international capital, has taken over the role of the iconic symbolism that architecture once performed; that is, images and iconography are now found in media, in virtual reality, in conditions more easily undestood and consumed than in architecture. If architecture no longer provides the imagery but only the necessary infrastructural needs

for international capital, how does it serve any ideological or critical function? This might be one of the discourses that would be possible for a critical architecture in a geopolitical world. One way architecture can again serve an ideological and critical function is to begin to loosen the notion of desire from the idea of grounding and locating. Today architecture accommodates, ameliorates and provides for all of those things that international capital desires; it is again another sequence of desire. Piranesi's drawings loosen the notion of architecture as a desire for ground because they no longer present the ground as a condition of its being. And if architecture no longer presents itself as a grounded condition, as a condition of being, then this opens the interiority of architecture to many possibilities.

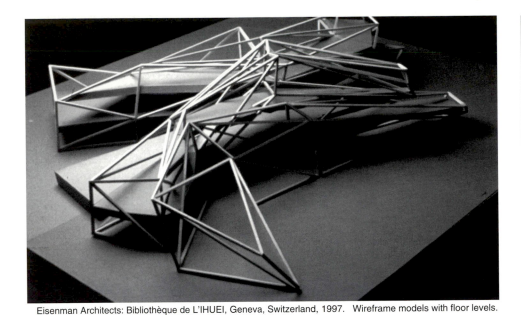

Eisenman Architects: Bibliothèque de L'IHUEI, Geneva, Switzerland, 1997.   Wireframe models with floor levels.

Model, 1:200 overhead view.

There has been a rupture in the continuous notion of history, in the shift from the notion of ideological politics to international capital. A similar rupture motivated Piranesi, in the movement from the hierarchies of the "*ancient regime*" to an ideological politics. Both of these fractures are seen within a discourse of an extensive view of a space-time continuum. If, instead, architecture is seen as an intensive condition that has been repressed within such an extensive view, then it might be possible to see in the alternatives to figure-figure urbanism, a way of deploying urban space and ground that provides a shift in the conditions of urban life. With the increasing number of one-person households, with home offices on line, there is no longer a series of deterministic desires for conditions of home, of office, of public space. These ideas have already become loosened from the desire for ground. Our unwillingness to see that this loosening has already occured is witness to the power that this idea has over us. A figure-figure urbanism is one critical possibility among many, that perhaps lies repressed in the idea of an ungrounded architecture.

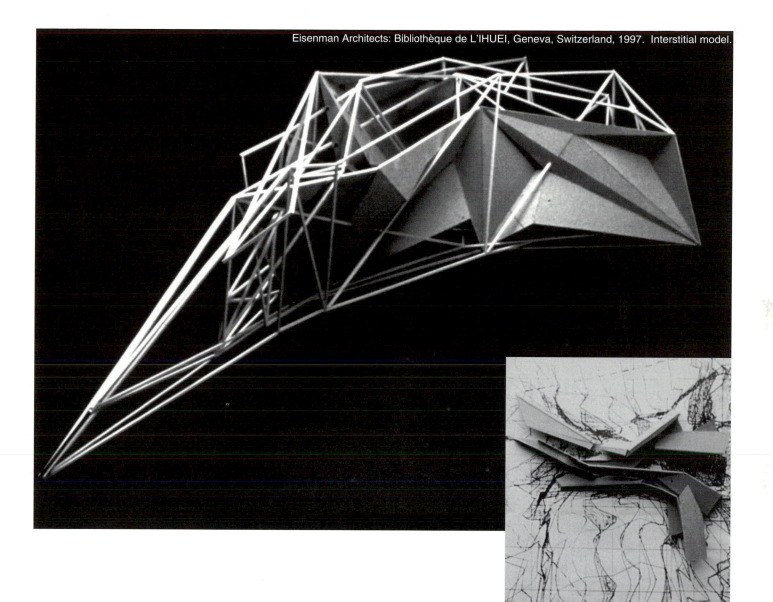

Eisenman Architects: Bibliothèque de L'IHUEI, Geneva, Switzerland, 1997. Interstitial model.

Study model.

Eisenman Architects: Church of the Year 2000, 1996. Model.

Rendering.

Model.

Eisenman Architects: Church of the Year 2000, 1996. Model.

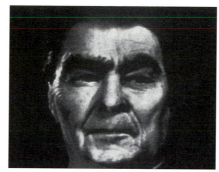
Warheads II. Nancy Burson, artist.

WILLIAM MACDONALD AND SULAN KOLATAN: RECENT WORK

CHIMERA FORMATIONS AND CO-CITATIONS

The collaborative projects of Kolatan/MacDonald selected for this portfolio are of entirely different scales and situations, each one addressing a series of issues. Observed together, they reflect our interest in the implications of new technologies for the discipline of architecture. The computer possesses a paradoxical capacity to be simultaneously instrumental and spatial. Thus its introduction into the field of architecture begs for a reevaluation of preexisting design methodologies and of inherited notions as to the nature and limitations of space. The projects illustrated each explore this ambiguity to varying degrees, and with varying emphasis on program and morphology.

One of the emerging spatial paradigms is that of the network as a system of interrelations between dissipative processes and aggregative structures that shape new spatial patterns and protocols. How does this network logic affect space and its making? Our work focuses in particular on the network model's capacity to facilitate cross-categorical and cross-scalar couplings whereby the initial systems/morphologies are not merely interconnected, but form new hybrid identities. What

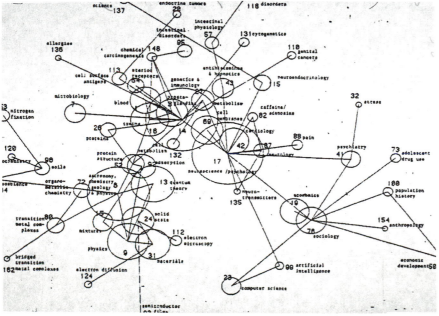
Co-Citation map.
Illustration from: "Mapping the Social Sciences: The Contribution of Technology to Information Retrieval." E. Garfield, R. Kimbeley, D.A. Pendlebury.

differentiates this new generation of chimerical hybrids from previous mechanistic ones is the act of transformation. These new systems are not determined and cannot be understood through a logical extension of the initial parts alone. They are hybrid, but nonetheless seamlessly and inextricably continuous.

The two specific models of the network and the hybrid that are of interest here are the co-citation map and the chimera.

Co-citation Mapping

This is a form of electronic indexing and information retrieval based on co-citation. "The principle underlying citation indexing is as follows: if one paper cites an earlier publication, they bear a conceptual relationship to one another. The references given in a publication thus serve to link that publication to earlier knowledge. Implicit in these linkages is a relatedness of intellectual content. In reordering the literature by works cited, we obtain a citation index."[1]

As an index, it functions according to a principle similar to that used in any keyword-based library search. Listing all works related to the same keyword, it reveals nonapparent conceptual connections across categories such as humanities and science. Interestingly, the next level of organization is constructed as a map, a geographic description of relational knowledge. In this kind of map, groups of co-cited papers are organized in clusters, each cluster representing a network of interrelated, co-cited publications. There are five iterations of increasing levels of networks in all. "What is achieved in clustering is a matrix of objects linked together by varying degrees and in different states of aggregation." [2] The graphic tool used for these maps is known as similarity mapping.

The co-citation maps have no absolute axis. Instead their spatial organization is based on continually evolving hierarchies that are contingent upon frequency of citation and thus subject to change over time.

(The) Chimera

The Chimera is the proper name given to a mythological monster, the "supreme hybrid," [3] constituted of part lion, part goat, part snake. Chimera, referred to as mosaicism, also denotes a pathological condition that occurs either spontaneously or is produced artificially, and in which individuals are composed of diverse genetic parts. Robert Rosen, in his essay "Cooperation and Chimera," notes that "chimera formation, in which a new individual, or a new identity, arises out of other, initially independent individuals, is a kind of inverse process to differentiation, in which a single initial individual spawns many diverse individuals, or in which one part of a single individual becomes different from other parts." [4]

If one replaces "individual" with "system" in the above statement, it becomes possible to situate the concept of chimera outside the realm of biology. In fact, Rosen goes on to assert that ecosystems and man-machine interactions are chimerical.

The chimerical differs in crucial ways from other forms of hybrid systems such as collage, montage or the prosthetic. While the latter are also systems in which the diverse parts operate together, these parts never lose their individual identities. In fact, the individual identity of each part, specifically the (categorical) difference, is more pronounced in systems based on strategies of juxtaposition or superimposition. And because each part exists as a discrete entity linked to other discrete entities, the whole can be taken apart. The idea of irreversible, irreducible hybridity both as concept and product would not have been thinkable within the paradigm of mechanics to which the techniques of collage and montage are linked.

In a chimera, the relationship between the constituent parts is not one of interconnection or adjacency. At least, not simply. The limits of the parts, the exact delineations of the thresholds between parts, are not clearly identifiable. Rather, like the result of a succesful graft, the border disappears. Locally, the part that was different becomes inextricably bonded with the rest.

One of the most interesting aspects of the concept of chimera occurs at a systemic level—namely, its ability to produce entirely new systems out of multiple hybrid configurations. These new systems are not determined and cannot be understood through a logical extension of only the initial parts.

Finally, and as a consequence of the first two points, a third aspect of the chimerical is that it is not reducible to its constituent parts. We have two primary interests in the chimerical. One has to do with its seeming capability as a concept to help define existing phenomena of fairly complex hybridity in which categorically different systems somehow operate as a single identity. The other is based on the assumption that the ways in which chimera are constituted and operate hold clues to a transformatively aggregative model of construction/production, that is, an aggregation that becomes more than the sum of its parts, and therefore is not reducible to its constituent parts. Thus, the chimerical has the potential to be both an analytical and a methodological tool.

In combination, the two models offer an opportunity to link dissipative/aggregative operations to transformative ones—the co-citation analog identifying similarities between unrelated sites/structures/programs, and the chimerical analog employing these initial similarities to construct new sites/structures/programs.

This attempt at constructing a methodology takes its cues both from the particular logic of the computer as well as from certain urban default conditions that we see happening today.

As exisiting building types and corresponding program entities are pulled apart through the combined effects of transportation/communication, the clusters emerging by way of this process can remain unattached, free agents as it were, or reaggregate—driven by opportunity or pragmatism—in unprecedented ways into new composite entities. It is through transformative operations that the aggregation of distinct parts obtains the qualities of continuity without necessarily again becoming a totalizing whole.

What are the spatial protocols operating here? Does this logic of particularization/aggregation offer clues for alternative theories of the city? And, how, if at all, is the traditional idea of built structures as discrete units intended for specific purposes still tenable under these circumstances?

What is at stake here, in a more general sense, is the concept of architectural and urban categorization that depends on the ability to clearly identify discrete elements/units/types. While existing categories might cease to be useful, the paradigm of the network/chimera has the potential to open up an entirely new range of previously inconceivable kinds of structures for which no names exist yet.

NOTES
1. E. Garfield, R. Kimbeley, D.A. Pendlebury, "Mapping the Social Sciences: The Contribution of Technology to Information Retrieval."

2. Ibid.

3. Michael Feher, ed, with Ramona Naddaff and Nadia Tazi, *The Chimera Herself. Ginevra Bompiano in Fragments for a History of the Human Body, Part One* (New York: Zone, 1989), 373.

4. Robert Rosen, "Cooperation and Chimera," in John L. Casti and Anders Karlquist, eds., *Cooperation and Conflict in General Evolutionary Processes* (New York: John Wiley and Sons, 1995), 343–44.

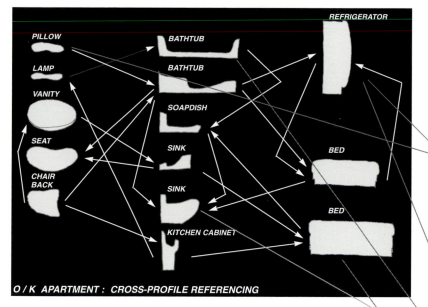

O / K APARTMENT : CROSS-PROFILE REFERENCING

Labels in image: REFRIGERATOR, PILLOW, BATHTUB, LAMP, BATHTUB, VANITY, SOAPDISH, SEAT, SINK, BED, CHAIR BACK, SINK, BED, KITCHEN CABINET

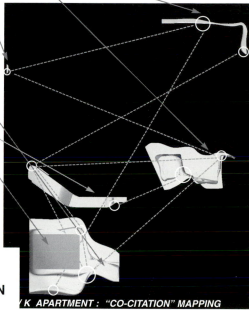

/K APARTMENT : "CO-CITATION" MAPPING

O/K Apartment. "Cross-profile"
referencing / "Co-Citation" mapping.

MORE THAN ONE/LESS THAN TWO RESIDENCE(S), 1997

This interior project was conceived somewhat in the manner of a "miniature urbanism" consisting of three phases: (1) identification of individual "sites" within the existing space (locations for new structures referred to as "domestic scapes"), (2) generation of these structures through cross-profiling and (3) mapping of similarities akin to co-citation mapping.

For the generation of the new structures on each site, section profiles of everyday domestic objects and furnishings were electronically cross-referenced to one another regardless of original scale and category but with an interest in registering formal and operational similarities between them. Based on this information, they were then spatially organized and resurfaced. The resulting structures are chimerical in the sense that the initial profiles as indexes of particular identities (bed, sink, sofa) are now inextricably embedded within an entirely new entity that they have helped produce. We will loosely refer to this new entity as a

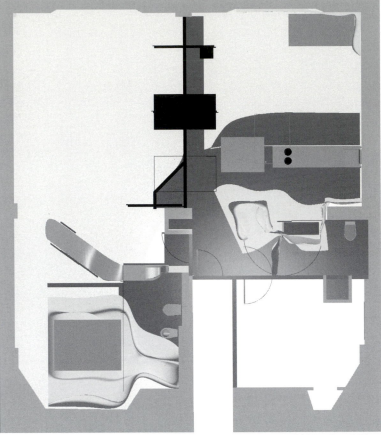

O/K Apartment. Plan.

"domestic scape," or synthetic topography. The "domestic scape," unlike the domestic space (the room) or the domestic object (the piece of furniture), cannot be sufficiently identified by categorization. Rather, like a particular landscape, its identification is contingent on the presence of a set of idiosyncratic features. As the discussion of identity is linked here to the question of programmatic performance, it is useful to continue the landscape analogy in evaluating the synthetic topography. In the case of the bed, for example a "plateau" measuring a minimum of 60 x 80" can be indentified, as but is not limited to a potential,sleeping area. This is very different from the concept of a "bedroom" or a "bed," which are both categorical designations of identity, and therefore fixed in their programmatic associations.

The formal and programmatic conditions thus obtained are unknown and impossible to preconceive or predict. The excess of (in)formation poses an interesting problem inasmuch as it is ambiguous and therefore open to interpretation on many levels. The resulting synthetic topographies, unlike conventional subdivisions by rooms, do not register legible distinctions between spaces or between programs. The "domestic scapes" are always situated across the boundaries of the existing

O/K Apartment. Perspective view of kitchen/bath area.

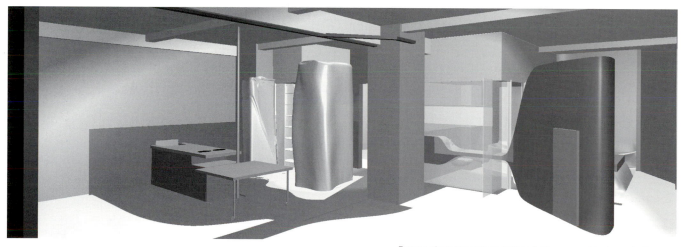

Perspective view toward kitchen/bath area and bedroom/bath area.

Longitudinal section: view east.

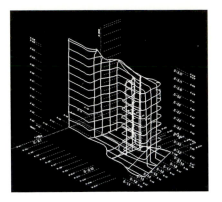
Isometric: kitchen/bath topography.

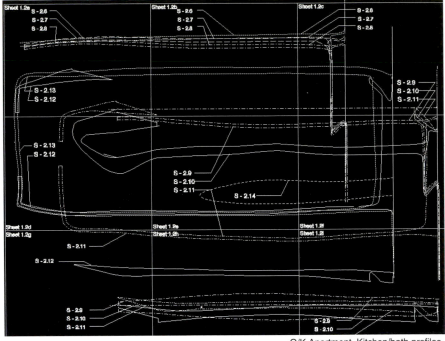
O/K Apartment. Kitchen/bath profiles.

Detail view of sink/medicine cabinet, Bath 1.

Detail view of sink/medicine cabinet, Bath1 and closet cabinet.

domestic spaces. The bed/bath scape, for example, forms a continuous surface within its own limits. One of the excesses produced here is the seamless transformation between the space shaped by the "bathtub" and the bedroom floor/wall. A door into the "bathtub" is sealed as the water level rises, pressing against it.

While the topographic model is useful in understanding certain aspects of these structures, it is important to note that the surface in this case is not just terrain—a top layer with a fairly shallow sectional relief—but deep, both in a conceptual and literal sense. Conceptually, this term denotes the possibility of an increased range. The surface is not exclusively conceived as thin, shallow, external, but capable of incorporating degrees of cavitation, inclusion, thickening, 3D spatial enveloping, interiority and so on. Considered in this way, the relation between deep and shallow, space and surface, is defined not as a dichotomy but within the terms of transformation. It is this capacity of the scape to change incrementally and continuously that produces a chimerical condition between furniture, space and surface.

Conventional assumptions about the codification of the interior surfaces as floors, walls and ceilings do not always hold here.

At the very least, the place and manner in which these constituent elements meet is redefined. In fact, they no longer meet.

SITING CO-CITATION
In the final phase of the project, these individual scapes are interconnected across the space of the apartment in a manner similar to co-citation mapping (electronic literary indexing). This kind of similarity mapping yields both an analysis of already existing relations—by indicating the co-presence of certain idiosyncracies across or regardless of type—relational method of production that

O/K Apartment. Longitudinal section: perspective view east.

Transverse section: view east at bedroom.

O/K Apartment. Plan.

Bed/bath under construction in factory.

Bed/bath under construction in factory.

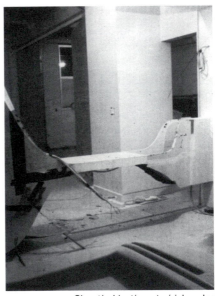

Closet/cabinet/counter/sink under construction on site.

produces simultaneous effects across an established network. An electronic web of second-iteration sites is constructed with the intent of mapping similarities and differences between heretofore unrelated entities. The individual sites are bound together as a system in which small-scale manipulations affect changes throughout, at varying scales and locales.

Team: Sulan Kolatan/ William J. MacDonald, with Erich Schonenberger, Natasha Cunningham, Rebecca Carpenter, Matt Hollis, Steve Doub and Phillip Palmgren.

Bath/bed under construction on site.

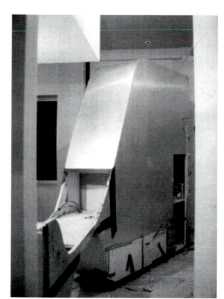

O/K Apartment. Counter/closet cabinet under construction on site.

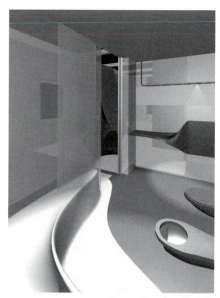

Perspective view, Bath 1.

Kitchen/shower under construction in factory.

Perspective view west toward glass bathroom wall and closet/cabinet.

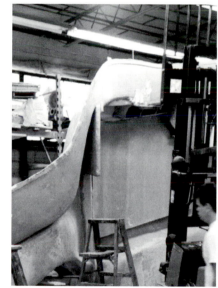

Bed/bath under construction in factory.

Perspective view, Bath 2.

Yokohama Port Terminal. "Horseshoe" Transformations.

YOKOHAMA PORT TERMINAL, 1994
Smale's Horseshoe Transformations

To make a sample version of Smale's horseshoe, you take a rectangle and squeeze it top and bottom into a horizontal bar.Take one end of the bar and fold it and stretch it around the other, making a c-shape horseshoe. Then imagine the horseshoe embedded in a new rectangle and repeat the same transformation, shrinking and folding and stretching. The process mimics the work of a mechanical taffy maker, with rotating arms that stretch the taffy, double it up, stretch it again, and so until the taffy's surface has become very long, very thin, and intricately self-embedded...

—James Gleick, *Chaos*

The spatial and structural attributes of the Yokohama Port Terminal Project were generated from digital operations very similar to the transformations described above. Our interest in these transformations was twofold. First, we were interested in a morphology of the very long, very thin and intricately self-embedded—possibly as a way of searching for an alternative paradigm to the banality of the ubiquitous very long, very low container building-type—and second, in the conceptual and programmatic potential of producing continual and unpredictable "neighborhood" changes throughout the structure.

As the location of individual points moves about in the various stages of Smale's Horseshoe Transformations, "local neighborhoods" are continually redefined and recombined.

Multiple Continuities

The third aspect of the project, which is linked to the first two, concerns a significant shift in the relation between the entire structure as a "whole" and its sections, and involves a kind of inverse sequencing of typical architectural design practices.

The customary sequence of operations proceeds from plan to section, establishing a single

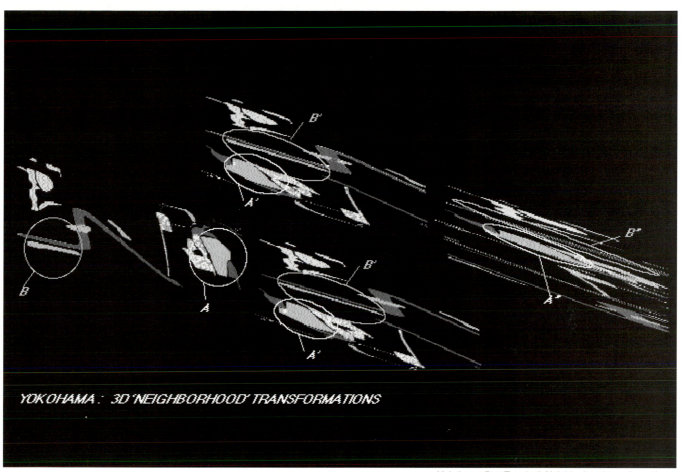

YOKOHAMA : 3D 'NEIGHBORHOOD' TRANSFORMATIONS

Yokohama Port Terminal. Neighborhood transformations.

Perspective of roofscape terraces with view toward entry road and the city of Yokohama.

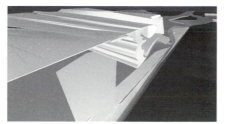

Detail perspective of Customs / Immigration / Quarantine view toward entry road.

continuity from the outset, whereafter the sections serve to document and confirm moments of that initial continuum. If, however, the process is initiated through a series of section cuts, as was done in this case, in which the digital transformations were employed to generate the sections, it is possible to conceive of multiple continuities moving through these cuts and connecting them, even if as a matter of course only one of these continuities is finally selected. Rather than privileging the ground-floor plan, from which everything else is consequently built up, and which frames all subsequent operations, this process implies a radically different concept of the plan to section—and, by extension, depth to surface—interconnection.

Deep Skin

This method produces, among other results, a kind of "deep skin" condition. On the one hand, the initial codification of the sections' digital cross-grain with exterior and interior programs, inextricably and repeatedly embeds the exterior within (more than 50 percent of the terminal program is comprised of outdoor functions). On the other hand, the process of gradual transformation from section to plan makes it difficult to distinguish between structure and skin. Horizontal and vertical cuts through the final structure show differences in degrees, instead of categorical differences, as is typically the case between plan and section. In fact, sections taken through the structure at any angle will appear as transformations of one another. The building's material thickens and thins in all directions, indicating structural qualities in some places and membrane-like qualities in others.

What is interesting here is an emphasis on thickness, as well as enveloping, that is, a three-dimensional, space-shaping quality of surface. This is a concept of skin that is not the opposite of deep—not "skin deep" as it were, but deep skin.

Conceived and made as accretive convoluted layers, skin and space are inextricable, and their relationship is no longer reducible to a simple hierarchy of container-contained.

Glossary

"Twisters:" Recurrent singularities in the surface/space/structure that are twisted; locations of level changes.

"Movers:" A secondary architecture of conveyors, escalators and conduits providing the speedy circulation of people, luggage, air, water and so on.

"Footholds:" Prepared micro-places such as outlets, brackets, anchors, taps, sockets and locks; part of a field of the same, dispersed across and located on all surfaces for eventual or immediate furnishing, wiring, planting and so on.

Yokohama Port Terminal. Elevation looking east.

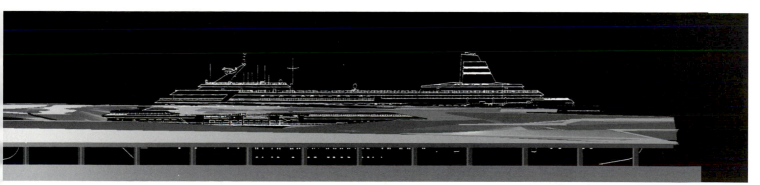

Elevation looking west.

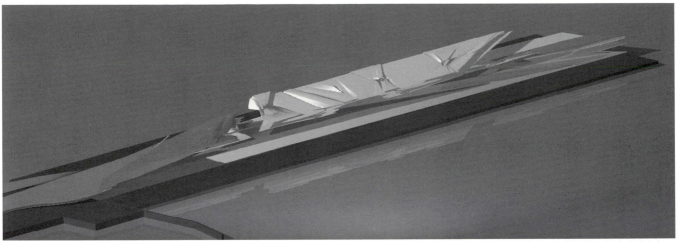

Yokohama Port Terminal. Aerial view.

Plan of roof-level garden and terraces.

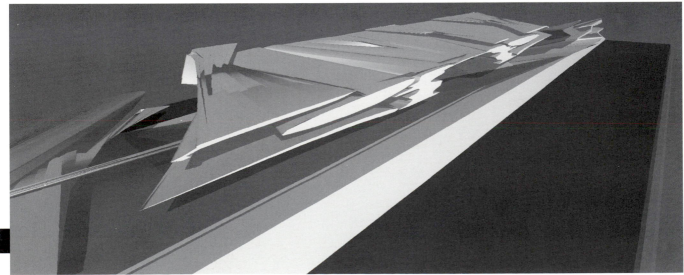

Aerial perspective view from the city of Yokohama toward the terminal.

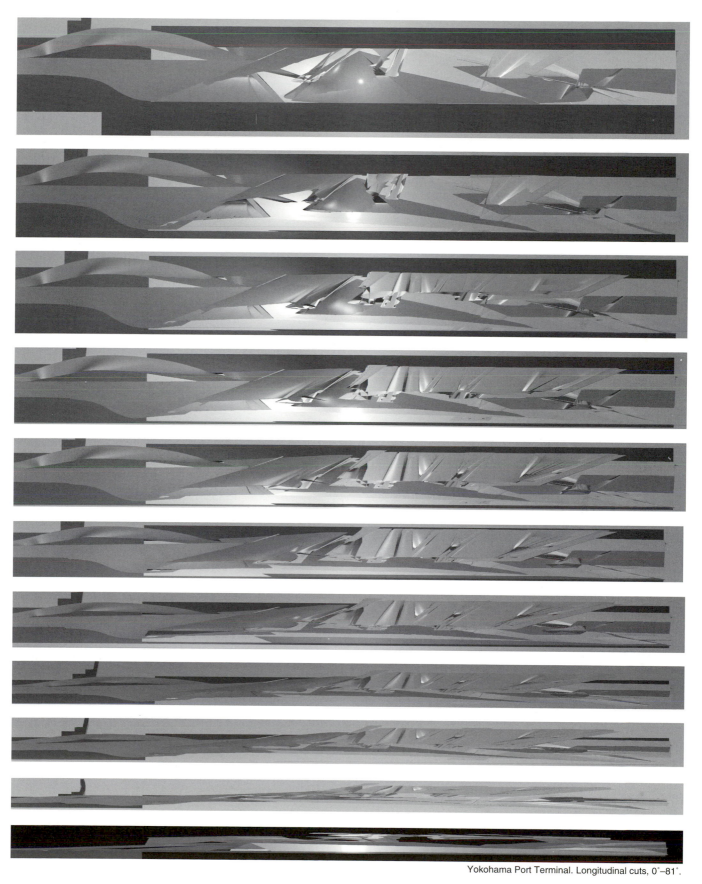

Yokohama Port Terminal. Longitudinal cuts, 0°–81°.

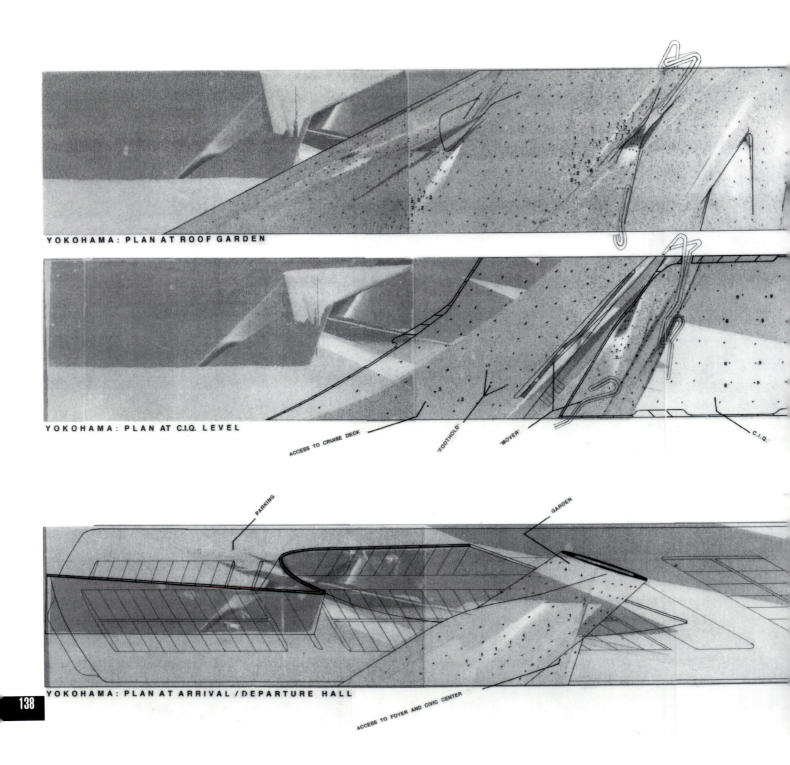

YOKOHAMA: PLAN AT ROOF GARDEN

YOKOHAMA: PLAN AT C.I.Q. LEVEL

ACCESS TO CRUISE DECK

'FOOTHOLD'

'MOVER'

C.I.Q.

PARKING

GARDEN

YOKOHAMA: PLAN AT ARRIVAL/DEPARTURE HALL

ACCESS TO FOYER AND CIVIC CENTER

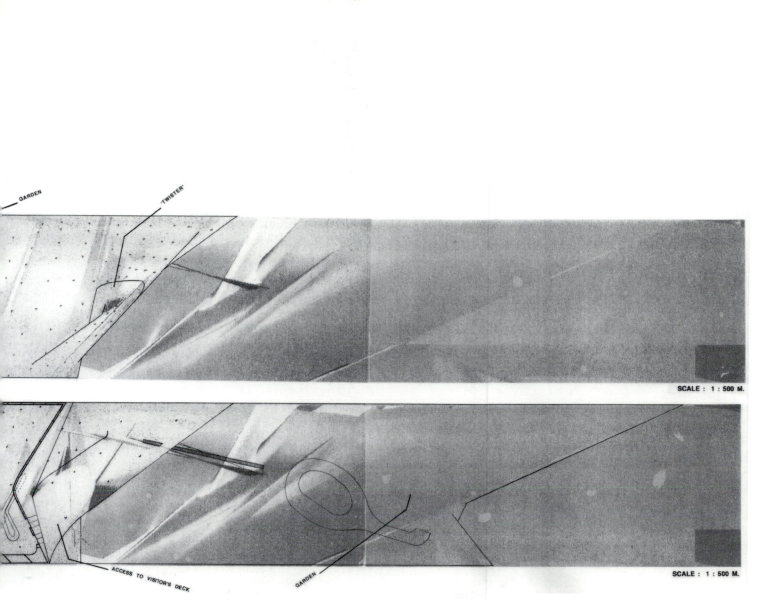

GARDEN

'TWISTER'

SCALE : 1 : 500 M.

ACCESS TO VISITOR'S DECK

GARDEN

SCALE : 1 : 500 M.

Yokohama Port Terminal. Plan at roof garden and at Customs, Immigration and Quarantine level .

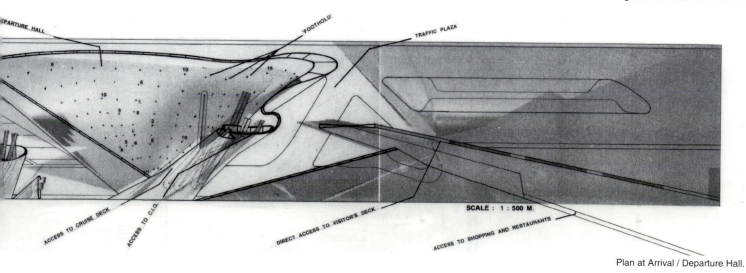

DEPARTURE HALL

'FOOTHOLD'

TRAFFIC PLAZA

SCALE : 1 : 500 M.

ACCESS TO CRUISE DECK

ACCESS TO C.I.Q.

DIRECT ACCESS TO VISITOR'S DECK

ACCESS TO SHOPPING AND RESTAURANTS

Plan at Arrival / Departure Hall.

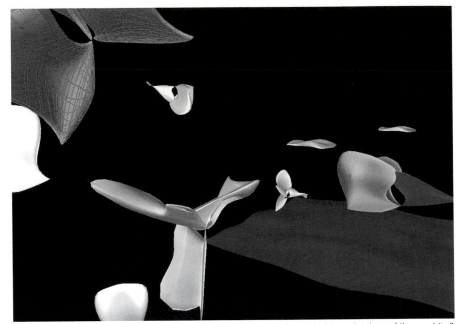

"lobbyingforbitparts." Perspective view of three "lounge bits" to be constructed out of fiberglass for the lobby of the Angelika Film Center, New York.

"lobbyingforbitparts." Chimerical investigations of "lounge bits."

Play

We propose a new form of cine-play for the Angelika Film Center. The playing field is constructed across several categories of site: the film theater, the lobby, the sidewalk, the home and the Web. The pieces of play are miscellaneous bits of film scanned into the lobby and the sidewalk on micro-monitors, and into the Web. The rules of play are derived from a limited number of spatial and temporal conventions of film, architecture, the telephone and the Internet. The players include theater audiences, idle crowds in the lobby, ticket buyers, passersby on the sidewalk and homebodies. Playtimes are during preview intervals in the theater, between opening and closing hours in the lobby and twenty-four hours a day in all other locations. The goals of play are contingent upon the siting of the player at a particular time. On the Web: to produce "spin-off" narratives of the film by employing its bits and adding personal minutiae to it through a storyboard/hypermedia format. In the lobby: to scan and review the film bits and lobby over the telephone with other players on and off the Web for selected bits. In the theater: to preview the latest spin-off narratives of the film.

Loop

Full-screen video cameras are mounted in three of the theaters and are adjusted to maximum close-up. They can be steered across the surface of the projected image via remote controls located in the lobby. These scanned 8 x 8" film bits appear on small monitors, also available in the lobby. While these monitors show continuous film bits simultaneously with the screening of the film, some of the

Duchesse. A Sheraton chaise lounge in one piece. It is described by the designer as two bergères with a footstool in the middle.

"lobbyingforbitparts." Perspective view of all five "lounge bits" to be constructed in fiberglass for the lobby of the Angelika Film Center.

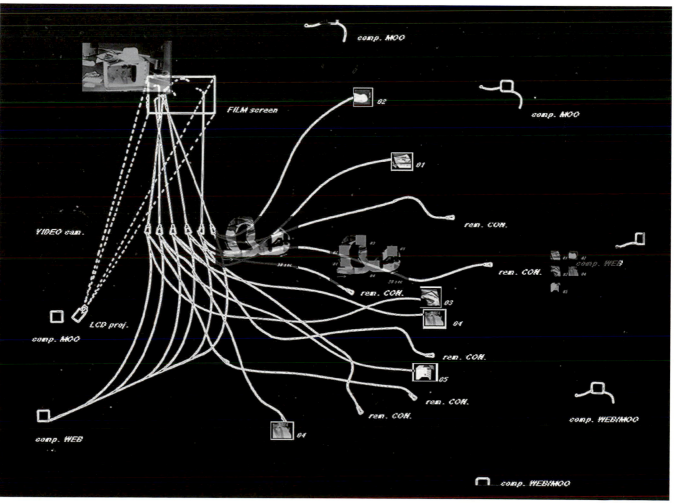

Co-Citation map.

"lobbyingforbitparts." Film bits format made available via the WWW "webbits" home page.

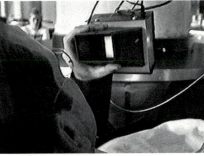

Device used for scanning cinema screens.

Lobbyist lobbying in the lobby.

"Lounge bit."

Cinema with "webbits" projections on cinema screen.

heaven says "So, this conversation is being projected."
thing says "Yep, that's what they've told me...."
heaven . o O (I guess I should be on my best behavior...

"Webbits." Simultaneous connection / projection of both text- (MUD) and image- (WWW) based environments on the cinema screen.

images are selected by a computer at intervals and placed into a Web site for extended play with a new set of players. A second Web location exists as part of a Multi-User Domain, or MUD. This conversational format may be used in combination with the image site. A second computer captures the activities on the Web sites and projects portions of them back onto the screen of a fourth theater before the previews.

Lounge

A playing lounge is constructed in the lobby bit by bit. The specific parts employed were selected from a scanning of bits from the cinema furniture (seats, backs of seats, arms of seats). These bits were then transformed according to computational techniques derived from familiar lounge-chair types (such as the "chair-and-a-half," the "watcher's chair," the "roundabout" and others). These normative samples were altered via computer through deformative operations such as scaling, splitting, doubling, tripling and rotating and "splined" with the columns in the space. The transformed bits are more than furniture, less than architecture. Their use, as well as their relation to the "floating" remote controls and the monitors carrying the film bits, are left undefined so as to be invented by the players.

ROUNDABOUT

Roundabout. A nineteenth-century three-seat unit. In plan, the three seats form a circle, and the three individual chair backs radiate and curve out from the central point of the circle. The seated persons must turn their heads toward the center of the circle to see and talk to others who are seated on the same piece of furniture.

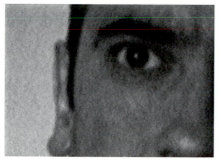
"lobbyingforbitparts." Scan of film from screen (8 x 8") as viewed from lobbyist's position.

Lobbyist lounging/scanning the cinema screen.

Lobbyist seated and scanning the cinema screen.

View of film from projection room.

Lobbyist scanning the cinema screen with remote control.

"Webbits" projected in cinema preceding the presentation of "actual" films, with an audience member in foreground.

DRUNKARD'S CHAIR

Drunkard's chair. Also called a "lover's chair." A Queen Anne–period trend that lasted through the eighteenth century. The seats were up to thirty three-inches wide, and allowed one person to sprawl comfortably, or two to nestle closely. In current usage it is sometimes referred to as a "chair-and-a-half."

(E)MERGE(D) STATE(S), 1992

INTRODUCTION
The territorial "order" between East and West was precisely demarcated by the physical presence of the Berlin Wall. Its eventual "actual" erasure was preceded/facilitated by the transgressive power of communication technologies.

Regarding this "effect" as symptomatic of the late twentieth century urban condition, the project attempts to formulate possible strategies for an urbanistic incorporation of communication/ transportation technologies. The project's domain includes the multiple (E)merged State(s) of East/West, public/politic, architecture/media and others.

The working process involved the examination of the city as an accumulation of interfacing network systems. Through precise local operations and situational interventions that support and extend existing practices, augmentative and new systems were implemented.

URBAN STRATEGY: SITE/CITY AND EAST/WEST OVERCONNECTION
Existing network systems of roads/river/long-distance/local tramway viaduct: East-West transportation linkages are reinforced and multiplied across the site. The Tiergarten extends as office-parkscape to Humboldt Hafen.

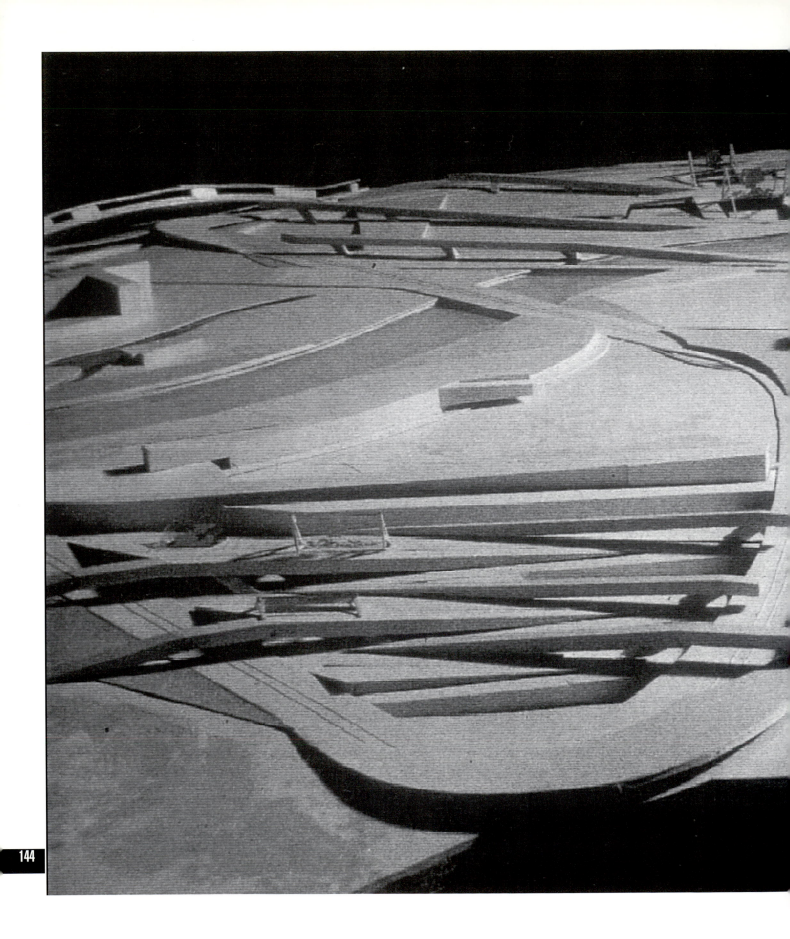

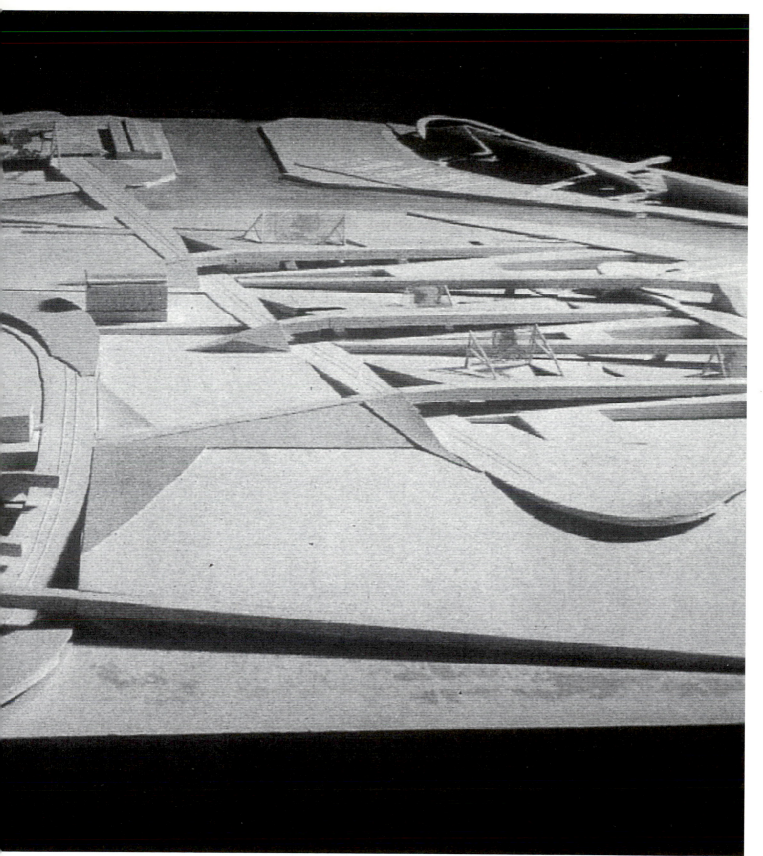

Competition project for German Parliament in Berlin. Overall view of model north from the Tiergarten.

Along the northern periphery these linkages aggregate programmatically and architecturally into complex multi-strand urban conduits (commercial/housing/retail/offices) to draw non-government-related activity to the site and promote public infiltration along the perforated viaduct. Strategically placed along the primary circulation through the site, the "elbow pit stop buildings" (tram stop/parking/small retail) tap into and facilitate everyday/every-night routines and encounters, between public and politic.

PROGRAMMATIC STRATEGY

It is hoped that this site becomes a field of government/ public/ media interaction with as much direct human and mediated contact as possible. Programatic inversions such as a politicized public/publicized politic, planned/unplanned encounters, politics/leisure, day/night functions and comfortable/ uncomfortable space are encouraged. The "politicized ground" is claimed through a modulated ground plane (sectionalized) that includes floating water lobbies, political arcades and political circuits.

Elements such as photovoltaeic fields, an inner-city wetland biotope and a wind (e)scape are integrated into the landscape.

SPATIAL STRATEGY

Through the merging of public park, architecture and media into an inextricably connected, heterogeneous and continuous scape, the constituent elements and inherent hierarchies of the normative government office building are "unraveled" and re-distributed within a non-hierarchical field. Planar and sectional manipulations of the ground enable polylateral spatial affiliations, both inside and

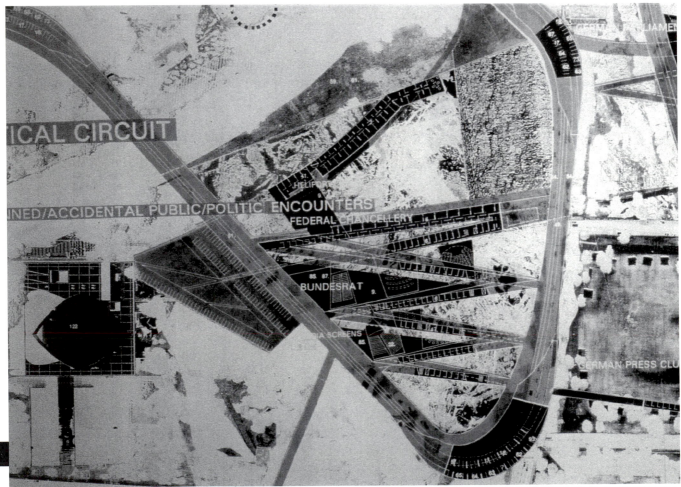

Competition project for German Parliament in Berlin. Detail of plan.

outside, while producing gradations of mediated/unmediated access between public and political territories. The media screens act as a ubiquitous fourth-wall condition. The warping ground allows for the absorption of scale from the existing iconographically bound structures. The interconnection between public and political programs continues across the "sponge buildings" by way of a transverse ground plane and mixed programming.

Competition project for German Parliament in Berlin. Detail of model. View east, overlooking the Platz der Republik/Reichstag.

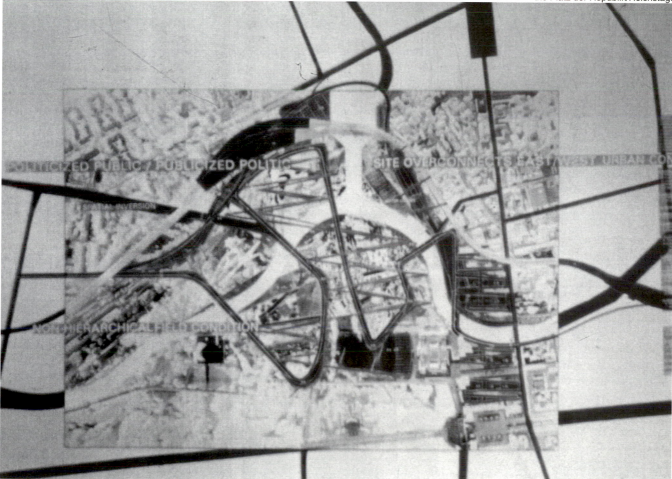

Competition project for German Parliament in Berlin. Urban plan.

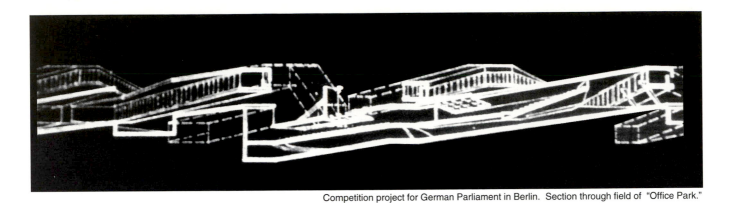

Competition project for German Parliament in Berlin. Section through field of "Office Park."

Glossary

POLITICAL CIRCUIT: An extension of east/west site overconnections. Derived from the automotive infrastructure (West) and the elaborate tramway infrastructure (East). The political circuit winds through the site as a local shuttle route linking all existing bridges, the Reichstag, Tiergarten entry, and planned tunnel entries, with local, mid-range and long-distance city/train/subway lanes.

The ELBOW PIT-STOP BUILDINGS: These edge the circuit, which through its composition provide for planned/accidental encounters between public and politic. Elbow pit-stop buildings are comprised of everyday/every-night functions, including daycare centers, bars, fast-food restaurants, sophisticated dining and dry cleaning. These structures consist of "peeling" the automotive road, simultaneously up and down, while the trains remain level. They provide parking above and below in addition to being major tram/auto stops on the political circuit. Due to the inhabitation of the automobile/tram triangular fields, these structures allow for the visual fields generated by the degrees of view possible via automobile/tram speeds relative to their positioning. These fields contain projection screens and leisure activities.

OFFICE PARK:
Refers to the distribution of the parliamentary and executive administration offices as bands through park and mediascapes. The arrangement of parliamentary offices is such that, due to security measures, parliament members occupy the bar flyovers while their administrative staff is placed under the shelf of the landscape, directly adjacent to the "media sleeve," which produces the "sectional cluster" of offices attained through the warped ground plane and the polylateral affiliations of space it allows. Entrances for offices open directly into a park- and mediascape.

SPONGE BUILDINGS:
Progammatically comprised of both commercial and political programs that are intended to increase and decrease as desire and need dictates. The structures are meant to accommodate these expanding and contracting programs via an internalized mobile facade, which itself is programmed with documentation/recording/ exhibition/ commercial functions. The relationship of these buildings to the field is best evidenced in their "scissors-like" sections that permit ground-to-roof access by tilting the ground plane. All entries are via this tilted ground plane.

NON-HIERARCHICAL FIELD CONDITION:
The modulation of ground plane, which affords the occupation of over/under surfaces, encompassing both the Bundestag and Bundesrat functions of the Parliament. The oversurface of the urban parkscape is intended to be randomly planted. The undersurface is comprised of meeting rooms and parking. Occupying the surface itself are the area's media sleeve and administrative offices and parliamentary offices that together comprise the sectional cluster distributions of office/meeting programs.

MULTI-STRAND URBAN CONDUITS:
Elliptical-chain structures that braid through the existing viaduct for trains. Programmatically, they consist of retail/commercial/housing/leisure activities as well as express-train and express-automobile routes from the Reichstag's Ufer to Moabit. The viaduct contains retail shops, open markets and public amenities.

COMFORTABLE/UNCOMFORTABLE SPACES:
Spaces with fluctuating identities that are triggered by programmatic or environmental changes. The daily temperature and velocity of the airflow through the windfunnel/windscape, for example, continually redefine the level of comfort at the site.

WATER LOBBIES:
Determined by a straightening of the width of the Spree River onto the site, which then becomes formal gardens for the arrival/departure of barges whose functions range from leisure (tourists) to political (lobbies that argue their case through sound and visual media on the water surrounding the Parliament).

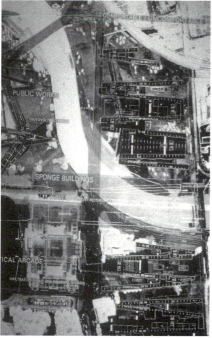

Competition project for German Parliament.
Detail plan of "sponge buidings" at Reichstag.

INNER-CITY WETLAND BIOTOPE:
The Tiergarten is the only real air exchange in Berlin and is not adequate for the purposes of the city. Our proposal extends the park from Unter den Linden to Humboldt Hafen and adds rainwater retainage lakes to increase the quality levels of the environment by creating an urban wetland biotope.

WIND FUNNEL/WIND ESCAPES:
Refers to the double-funnel-shaped portion of the political circuit that is outlined in evergreen trees. The double-funnel shape follows the planned tunnel below ground and also directs the natural winds from the south to the north and toward the Moabit sector to increase air speed and encourage air exchange.

PUBLIC WORKS:
Photovoltaeic fields with open-air markets (under) and additions to public infrastructure (both communication and transportation) are intended to inextricably link the parliament district to the public workings of the city. Also, the programmatic infrastructure is expanded by permitting the exchange of political program during the day for that of leisure programs at night and weekends, ensuring a twenty-four hour usage of the area.

EAST/WEST SITE OVERCONNECTIONS:
Major public infrastructural systems that have been adopted and adapted to emerge from the divorced areas of the city. These elements include the river, automotive arteries, communication infrastructure, tramways, trains (long-distance, medium-distance and inter/intra-city) and the parkscape and lakes, which are all thought to be an extension of public infrastructure .

POLITICAL ARCADE:
An integration of communication infrastructure and landscape such that the media screens that simultaneously broadcast political events (or entertainment advertising) are merged on the landscape of the non-hierarchical field. The screens are lifted into the vertical position only when in use, therefore the political activity or climate can be immediately assessed by the number and frequence of use; of these devices. The field is constantly in the state of becoming dependent upon the interaction of public and politic.

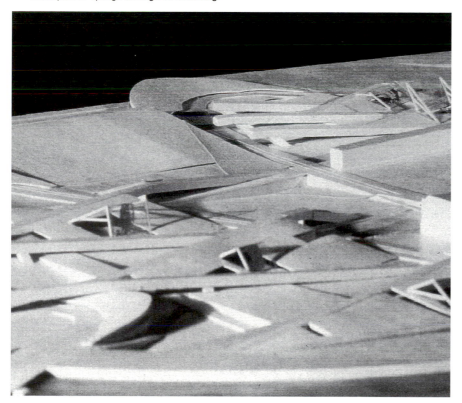

Competition project for German Parliament in Berlin. Detail of model (Bundesrat/Bundestag) looking south toward the Tiergarten.

Design Team: Ayse Sulan Kolatan / William J. MacDonald, Minsuk Cho, Ferda Kolatan and Chiakai Yang.

Collaborators: Anke Scheren, Michael Kennedy, George Grenier III, Joseph Bula, Bane Gaiser, Patrick Kane, Antonio Palladino, Teresa Chang, Gayle Tsem and George Krassas.

Special acknowledgment: Model Builders: Kennedy Fabrications +.

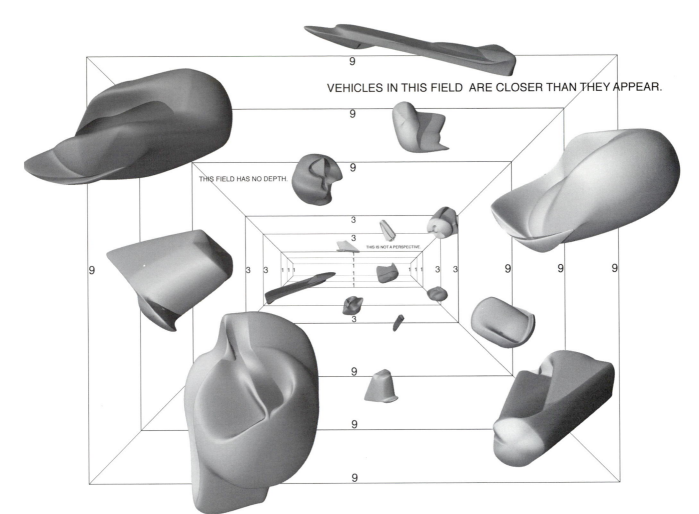

VEHICLES IN THIS FIELD ARE CLOSER THAN THEY APPEAR.

THIS FIELD HAS NO DEPTH.

THIS IS NOT A PERSPECTIVE.

INDEX OF RELATIVE VEHICLE SIZES *NO SCALE*

All vehicles.

VEHICLES, 1996

Read this information before using vehicles.

In her book entitled *On Longing,* Susan Stewart notes that "the metaphors of the book are metaphors of containment, of exteriority and interiority, of surface and depth, of covering and exposure, of taking apart and putting together."[1]

The metaphors of the box, like those of the book, are metaphors of containment and miniature. The vehicle, on the other hand, represents a self-contained world while at the same time availing itself as a means of transport. The car and the computer terminal are two vehicles. This categorical doubling puts into question the metaphors of containment alluded to above.

The late twentieth century offers a proliferation of such vehicles, which at first glance appear to share certain attributes. First,

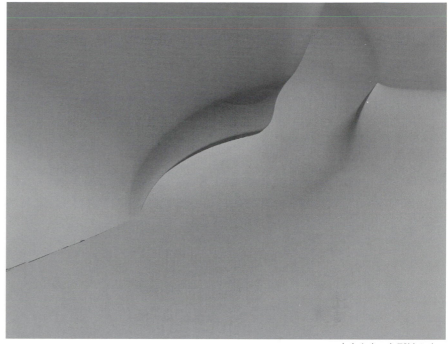

vhcl_4.size.d>72'-interior.

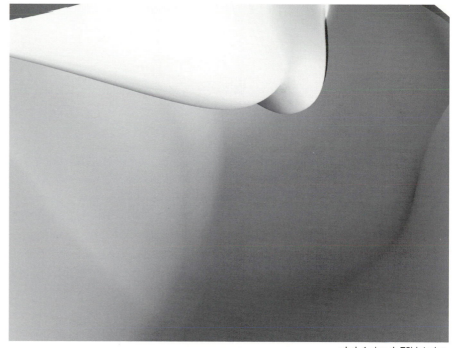

vhcl_1.size.d>72'-interior.

there is an implied interiority, whether it involves the actual provision of enclosure or merely the referencing of an intimate realm by operating within close range of the body. Second, these vehicular object/spaces display a distinctly "molded" morphology that in turn is linked to their relation to the human body, their ability to transport and the means of production from which they stem. Third, these vehicles are driven at high speed. Fourth, they are controlled by small,

vhcl_3.size.d>72'-interior.

semiautomatic bodily motions. On the other hand, the spaces across which they transport and the systems that bind them are gigantic in scale.

Frederic Jameson refers to this problem of incommensurability as the fundamental problem of form in the twentieth century. How is the relation between a large number of very small, very similar entities and colossal structures presently constructed? The miniature vehicle and the gigantic spatial structure are programmatically connected through artificially constructed protocols rather than through a container/contained relationship.

What other scenarios for this miniature/gigantic interdependency can be proposed? Can the colossal structure be conceived in terms of the small entities it contains?

Stewart notes that "the depiction of the miniature moves away from hierarchy and narrative in that it is caught in an infinity of descriptive gestures." Everything is made "to count" and nothing can be counted. It is interesting to note that this very definition of the miniature is by the same token a description of its monumentality.

It is important to distinguish here between size and scale. While

vhcl_6.size.c<36'.

152

vhcl_3.size.c<36".

vhcl_5.size.a<3".

vehicle vhcl_1.size.b<9".

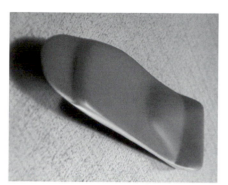

vhcl_3.size.c<36".

vhcl_4.size.a<3".

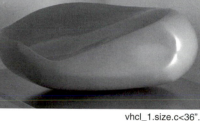

vhcl_1.size.c<36".

size denotes a quantitative material presence, scale, in Stewart's words, "is established by means of a set of correspondences to the familiar." In other words, while the size of an object or space always remains the same, its scale changes relative to its context. The extremely small, like the extremely large, turns an ordinary context into an extraordinary one. As such a vehicle of transformation of the everyday.

The vehicles are all built in different sizes as formally self-similar—similar in quality and quantity of articulation. Rather than possessing a predetermined scale or significance, the vehicle assumes a particular scale and significance in association with (m)any everyday context(s) or in relation to some other thing or space. This is not to say that it is neutral. On the contrary, it would be more accurate to describe it as a cumulative index of multiple codes. The initial generative information was assembled from a range of existing transportation/immersion vehicles and their codes and protocols. Each new vehicle was produced from several existing vehicular morphologies (such as mouse, receiver and car seat). Though the latter were selected from a multitude of scales, they were adjusted to one another in size, their particular hybridizations informed by qualitative coincidences of volume and surface articulations. (For some of these criteria, see tables.) The potential programmatic appropriation of these new vehicles, their new identity, as it were, is influenced in part by their performance value at varying scales and within various scenarios of interrelations of spaces and objects. One such possible scenario was constructed in the smaller room of an exhibition gallery. The vehicle was experienced by the visitor simultaneously as a small object on a table and a projected architectural interior (in reference to which the object could also be regarded as an exterior "model"). The same spatial arrangement appears to the eye of the camera as a considerably larger object sitting on what seems to be ground merging into the projected space. In addition to these two, there are other spatial layers to and from the vehicles Web site, as well as to the stage set, all of which converge into an extended feedback system.

Relations between vehicles, and between the vehicle and other items, including performances in the gallery and on the Web—the formerly contained—are not based on a preconceived hierarchy but on a more fluid concept of interorientation, an orientation without fixed axes, across a field of moving, interchanging or transforming references.

The vehicle is a player's item, a user's item and a collector's item. Operating in the capacity of varying agencies, it is simultaneously toy, prop, instrument, object and space.

154

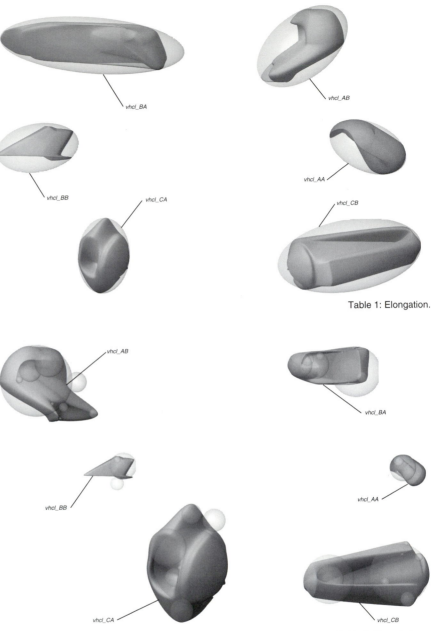

Table 1: Elongation.

Table 2: Roundedness.

Notes:
1. Susan Stewart, *On Longing* (Durham, N.C.: Duke University Press, 1993), 37.

2. Ibid, 47.

William MacDonald is associate assistant professor of architecture at Columbia University.

Sulan Kolatan is adjunct assistant professor of architecture at Columbia University. Both are principals of Kolatan/MacDonald Studio in New York City.

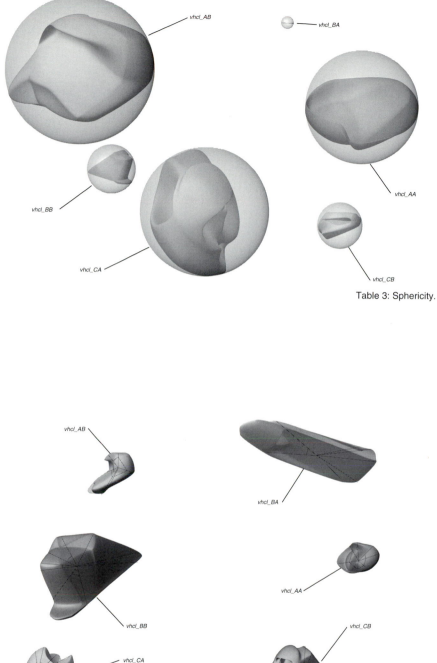

Table 3: Sphericity.

Table 4: Angularity.

The work presented in this article was on view at Columbia University's South Gallery, Buell Hall from February 18 to March 22, 1996.

With Erich Schoenenberger, Chris Perry, Cory Clarke and Philip Anzalone.

HAMLET:

Do you see yonder cloud that's almost in shape of a camel?

POLONIUS:

By the mass, and 'tis a camel, indeed.

HAMLET:

Methinks it is like a weasel.

POLONIUS:

It is backed like a weasel.

HAMLET:

Or like a whale?

POLONIUS:

Very like a whale.

Quotation from *The Shape of Powder-Particle Outlines*, by A. E. Hawkins.

JESSE REISER AND NANAKO UMEMOTO
RECENT WORK

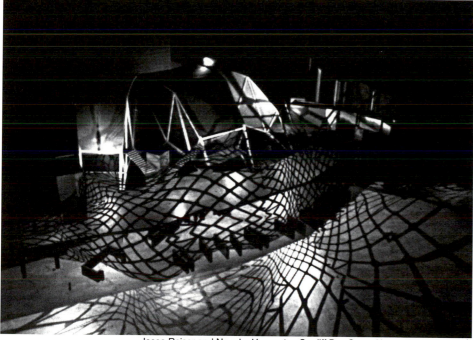

Jesse Reiser and Nanako Umemoto: Cardiff Bay Opera House, England, 1994.

BUILDING NOTES

Loose Fit

Seventy-six years ago, in the aftermath of the First World War, Paul Valéry, anticipating the triumph of the totalizing ideologies of modernity, wrote: "The world, which has given the name of 'progress' to its tendency towards a fatal precision, is seeking to unite the blessings of life with the advantages of death. A certain confusion still reigns; but yet a little while and all will be made clear; at last we shall behold the miracle of a strictly animal society, a perfect and final ant hill."[1]

This speculation was tragically borne out by the close of World War II, when modernism itself came to be implicated in the multiple horrors perpetrated by both the Right and the Left. These totalizing conceptions are very much with us—exponentially greater, in fact, in their reach and effects, than those of 1945.

How then to respond specifically within the purview of architecture? To renounce systematicity in an effort to become non-ideological, that is, to turn away from instrumental reason, is a stance of refusal that at best renders any architectural efforts ineffectual and at worst passively abets the consolidation of these totalizing conceptions. This does not mean to imply that there is a direct connection between a particular system, political or otherwise, and a particular architectural form. Indeed it is the very susceptibility of systems to transformation that suggests systematic inquiries into principles by which these transformations may be effected.

One promising line of development—and one that has begun to inform our work—has been the inquiry into chaotic or complex systems, especially their capacity to engender new and unforeseen formations of program, institutions and form. Central to this revaluation of system has been the attempt to rethink the nature and use of hierarchy in the design process, especially as it pertains to the complex exchanges between "given" systems within a context and how these shade into systems specific to the project itself.

In a discipline regulated by dualisms, four stand out. These are the assumed oppositions between theory and practice, structure and ornament, the global and the local and program and form. Our task, like that of our colleagues, entails a loosening of these polarities, first and foremost in the design process, and later as conclusions.

1. Theory and Practice: Theory cannot be privileged. It is neither superior to, nor above, practice. Neither philosophy nor history can legitimate the work of theory. Theory is not applied. On the contrary, theory occupies what Stan Allen describes as a "horizontal relation" to practice.

2. Structure and Ornament: Contrary to the classical formulation, ornament in not ornament at all but a more extensive and robust form of structure. This can be proved by the fact that ornament carries within itself the lineaments from which structure might be extracted. The reverse, however, is not possible.

3. The Global and the Local: The relationship between global systems of transport and exchange and specific or local architectural proposals have been understood (within modernism) as being mutually exclusive or in some dialectical relationship with one another. Our response is to propose architectures that would implicate one in the other and in so doing would attempt to bring about emergent or spontaneous events.

4. Program and Form: We acknowledge the loose fit between program and form and, following from this, the lack of priority of the former over the latter. This can be summed up in the analogy: "Program is to architecture what lyrics are to music." Indeed such correspondences might encompass a series of possible uses rather than define any one. The ancient and perhaps questionable analogy between forms of architecture and forms of music finds its most recent formulation in the loose fit between program and form. Loose fit of course involves a spectrum of congruencies ranging from the tight fit of the rhyming lyric to the loose fit of the dissonant one. In both cases, however, contingency is a fundamental condition as the rhyming or lack of rhyming is not in any meaningful way attached to the form.

If we cautiously approach any discussion of theory or method in direct relation to design, it is because linear develop-ments, while convenient for the sake of argument, rarely fit neatly or linearly into the event. All too often this apparent inevitability becomes visible only retrospectively and thus appears preordained though the actual working-out of the project was far messier. Such a situation becomes exacerbated when issues of perception are thematic to the work; for acts of perception become

inextricably mixed with their representations. The clearest way out of this impasse is to focus not on representation and issues of meaning, but on the organization of the work and its effects. In this regard the diagrammatic organization can be liberated from the meaning and intentionalities that might have prompted them; the work thus will always engender more meaning and find more unanticipated uses than is predicted within the confines of the concept.

Ornament and Conformity
Prominent among the dualisms that have regulated Western architectural thought has been the opposition between ornament and structure. Certainly within the tendencies that may be associated with modernism, this opposition has reached a critical and even apocalyptic state. The most radical formulations attempt to erase one of the terms of the opposition (ornament), with the consequent movement of ornament into a covert or recessive condition within the prevailing structure. Postmodern practice, especially the historicist branch, promised to resuscitate ornament in response to what was perceived to be the sterility of a homogeneous modernism. Those practices, however, continued to uphold both aspects of the classical relationship, the oppositional and the hierarchic dominance of structure over ornament: in historicism, by detaching ornament from structure as a form of pastiche signage; and in (latter-day) modernism, by reenacting the structure/ornament heirarchy—regular structure becomes a limiting and regulating framework for interstructural screens, upon which (electronic) media is projected.

New architectural potentials arise out of a fundamental reappraisal of the status of ornament and its implications for architectural organization. Axiomatic to this approach is the critique, and ultimately the dismantling, of the dualistic structure that has heretofore regulated these conceptions. First and foremost, we must assume, contrary to the classical formulation, that ornament is not subservient to structure but that, in fact, ornament is preeminently structure in itself. Furthermore, we acknowledge that what would classically be understood as structure falls within the general ornamental organization. This collapsing of the dichotomy has potentially far-reaching architectural consequences—though not, as one might immediately suppose, as a vehicle for producing yet another ornamentalized architecture. Rather, the ornamental is used as a graphic instrument capable of engendering complex organizations and spatialities, those that would foster unforeseen irruptions of institutional forms and programs.

From Type to Schema

Ever since Durand's "revolutionary" codification of formal types in his 1801 *Recueil et parallèle des édifices de tout genre, anciens et moderns*, architects of varied persuasions have been compelled to position themselves in relation to "the catalogue." At stake are issues still hotly contested today: Is it possible (or valuable) to exhaustively describe all that might legitimately fall within the compass of architecture? What is the relationship between the formal and the political—not simply the variable relation between a particular form and a particular political doctrine but perhaps more importantly, the assumed apoliticality or typology itself.

Divergent ideologies have sought to answer these questions within their own monolithic strictures. Critical and conservative agendas alike espouse a faith in a universal catalogue of formal types, undergirded by the platonic assumption of the existence of transhistorical models—static, hieratic and as yet uninfected by the particular accidents of site, program, materials and politics. (It is, of course, in their particular employments that the ideologies differ.) Novelty, if such a word can be used in this context, would be reserved only for the advent of a new type like the railroad terminal or the airport, which would then be added to the universal list. Type must be understood in a new way, by multiplying its conventional limits; or put another way, by encouraging a fundamental shift from type understood as the essential, static geometric lineament underlying building to type as a performative condition. In a convergence of flows of graduated scales and limits, type in the conventional sense represents but an artifact in a field in flux. Complexity theory provides a compelling model (and term) for this shift.

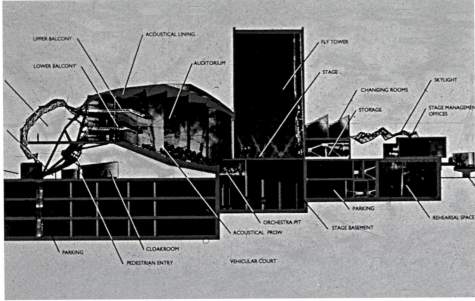

Cardiff Bay Opera House. Section.

CARDIFF BAY OPERA HOUSE

This project seeks to integrate the opera house into the unique historical and spatial configuration of Cardiff's inner harbor by constructing the project as a series of infrastructural events. Regarding the opera house infrastructurally enables us to redefine the nature and limits of the project at the extremes of scale, both as an integral part of the city and its environs and at the scale of the performance on stage. The opera house, therefore, is not understood as an isolated monument but as an open cultural form that embodies the same imperative and necessity of docks, tunnels and roads that structure the harbor itself.

Circulation

In keeping with the importance of infrastructure, the opera house site was organized according to three distinct patterns of pedestrian and vehicular access.

1. Pedestrian access from the oval piazza occurs at grade by way of direct entry into the concourse.
2. Automobile and taxi access is kept distinct from pedestrian access by linking Pierhead Street on the southeast side of the site with James Street on the northwest side, creating a vehicular court through the center of the site that allows ample covered drop-off and waiting areas along the inside face of the concourse. Access to underground parking is also from the vehicular court.
3. Truck delivery of sets and other large objects is made by way of a one-way elevated service road, entering from Pierhead Street— ramping up and following the northern edge of the site and ramping down to exit at James Street.

Public Programs

THE CONCOURSE/FOYER
The concourse/foyer component is seen as the crucial link between the

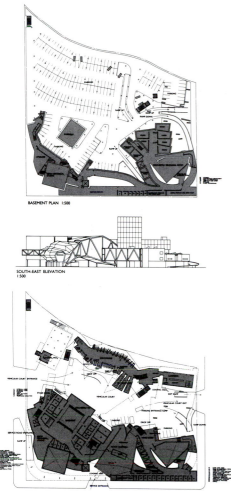

BASEMENT PLAN 1:500

SOUTH-EAST ELEVATION 1:500

GROUND FLOOR PLAN 1:500

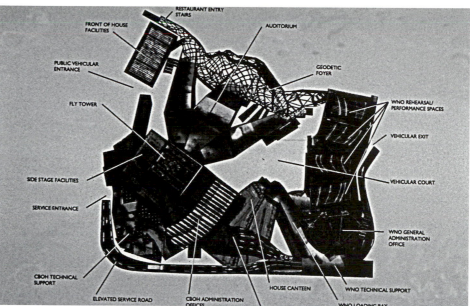

Cardiff Bay Opera House. Plan.

exterior public spaces and the events in the opera house complex. To this end we propose a form that would maximize transparency and exchange between piazza and concourse at the ground level and between auditorium and foyers above.

The geodetic "bag" that makes up the concourse/foyer is divided into three tubes that then insinuate themselves into the respective prongs of the theater "claw." These insinuations develop the lobby forms for the auditorium. Their meandering plan form permits a total continuity between foyer and auditorium that blocks sound and light transmission between the spaces. No doors are necessary. While extensively glazed on the exposed exterior surfaces, the surfacing of the "bag" becomes the acoustical lining of lobbies and the auditorium proper.

AUDITORIUM

The auditorium comprises three bridges, joined at one end, spanning the space between the stage/flytower volume and the concourse/foyer. The form of the auditorium is created by the desire to combine the advantages of intimacy and early lateral sound reflections, as provided in the traditional shoebox hall with, the significantly larger seating requirements of the brief.

To achieve this we have notionally joined together three shoebox halls, each splayed at angles. Two large prows are left at the joins to provide a large sound-reflecting side wall area for the rear seats, where the side walls of the three halls merge and disappear. The necessary lateral reflection to the central seats is provided by segmenting the main floor into three areas, with the second-level seating rising above the first-level seating. The step between the two levels forms a vertical sound-reflecting surface that provides early lateral sound energy to the seats on the first level.[2]

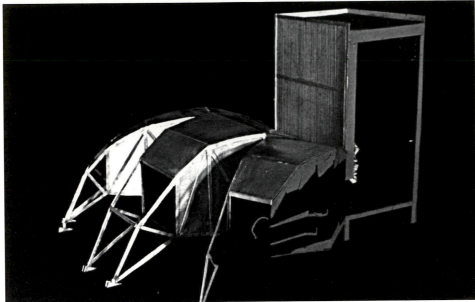

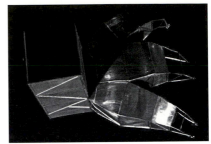

Cardiff Bay Opera House.
Claw/fly space system.

Cardiff Bay Opera House. Claw/fly space system.

REHERSAL SPACES

The rehearsal facilities for the Welsh National Opera are designed to allow for possibile simultaneous "in-house" and public performance. The configuration of four rehearsal spaces is inherently flexible, allowing them to be used independently, in conjunction with one another or as one large space. A steel roller blind curtain system creates the necessary movable partitions. The entire floor area is divided into eighty platforms. These can be moved hydraulically, enabling the topography of the floor to be infinitely variable, and to achieve virtually any form of theatrical arrangement of stage, platform, apron, seating rake, tower or terrain.

Some Notes on Geodetics

The current discussion regarding the tactics of achieving formal and programmatic heterogeneity in the realm of architecture and planning has occasioned a reassessment of spatial models and technologies that have heretofore been relegated to the scrap heap of utopian modernism. Such systems have come to be associated with the structures of a totalizing spatial ideology and an attempt to produce homogeneous and unified architectural languages.[3] Among these discarded technologies stands the geometric and structural conception known as geodesics (or geodetics).[4] Popularized by Buckminster Fuller and his followers as an architectural and urbanistic panacea, it is presently encountered in the occasional fairground structure or military installation (usually in the form of a dome). Geodesics has been detached from its utopian projections. This unfortunate history had served to obscure a prior and ironically more open set of possibilities in the field of descriptive morphology and aeronautics.

The structural system known as geodetics, developed by the English engineer Sir Barnes Wallis, was first used in the R-100 Airship, later in the Vickers Wellesley and, most

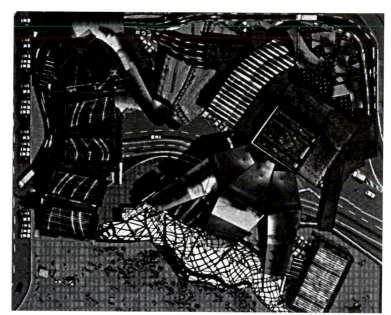

Cardiff Bay Opera House. Site plan.

famously in the Wellington Bomber. Geodetics derives from the Greek term *geodesis*, the imaginary geographical lines following the curvature of the earth along straight paths. The aim of the geodetic system is to carry all loads along the shortest possible paths; hence it produces a crisscross pattern of self-stabilizing members by means of which loads in any direction are automatically equalized by forces in the intersecting set of frames. This results in a structure that is extremely light and strong.[5] The durability is due in part to the inherent characteristic of extreme redundancy— if some portion of the structure is lost, the stresses are simply rerouted to the remaining members. Therefore, one can say that, in contrast to most conventional systems, the geodetic system is structurally diffuse, or nonessential.

A contemporary of Barnes Wallis (and possibly an influence) was the biologist D'Arcy Thompson, who, in his book *On Growth and Form* wrote the following:

> If we take any two points on a smooth curved surface, such as that of a sphere or a spheroid, and imagine a string stretched between them, we obtain what is known in mathematics as a "geodesic" curve. It is the shortest line which can be traced between the two points upon the surface itself, and it has always the same direction upon the surface to which it is confined; the most familiar of all cases, from which the name is derived, is that curve, or "rhumb-line," upon the earth's surface which the navigator learns to follow in the practice of "great-circle sailing," never altering his direction nor departing from his nearest road. Where the surface is spherical, the geodesic is literally a great circle, a circle, that is to say,

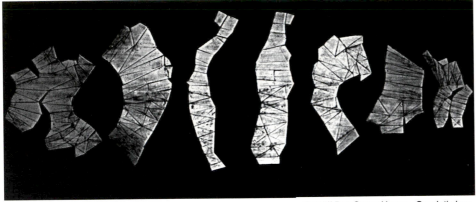

Cardiff Bay Opera House. Geodetic bag.

whose center is the center of the sphere. If instead of a sphere we be dealing with a spheroid, whether prolate or oblate (that is to say a figure of revolution in which an ellipse rotates about its long or its short axis), then the system of geodesics becomes more complicated. For in it the elliptic meridians are all geodesics, and so is the circle of the equator; though the circles of latitude are not so, any more than in the sphere. But a line which crosses the equator at an oblique angle, if it is to be geodesic, will go on so far and then turn back again, winding its way in a continual figure-of-eight curve between two extreme latitudes, as when we wind a ball of wool. To say, as we have done, that the geodesic is the shortest line between two points upon the surface, is as much to say that it is a *trace* of some particular straight line upon the surface in question, and it follows that, if any linear body be confined to that surface, while retaining a tendency to grow (save only for its confinement to that surface) in a straight line, the resultant form which it will assume will be that of a geodesic.[6]

As aviation technology, geodetics represents something of an anomaly— a short-lived tributary from mainstream technology, which tended increasingly toward stressed-skin construction. Though geodetics was a versatile system that could conform to the intricacies of aircraft configuration, it was typically cost-prohibitive due to its inherent complexity. In effect, each aircraft became a highly crafted object— which required special dies and jigs on which metal could be manually bent and formed for each strut.[7]

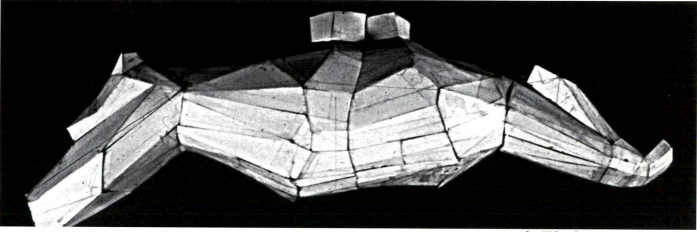

Cardiff Bay Opera House. Geodetic bag.

In an architectural context, however, given an interest in structural systems that might engender complexity through flexibility, geodetics becomes interesting precisely because as it is capable of adapting to complex spatial formations without a corresponding increase in the complexity of the system. In geodetics exact geometries such as the dome are no more ideal than any number of volumetric configurations. Moreover, the advent of computer-linked design and fabrication has obviated the technical difficulties encountered in earlier uses.

Among the properties and possibilities in a "supple" employment of geodetics are the following:

1. Geodetics, both historically and operationally, falls between two totalizing systems:

> A. The skeletal model: structure and skin.

> B. The structural skin model as a monocoque construction.[8]

Geodetics, on the other hand, acts as a structural tissue, or flesh—an intermediate structure capable of assembling heterogeneous agglomerations of space, program and path.

2. Geodetics is protean— in the sense that the structure can change and adapt to the space it develops by:

> A. Changing the fineness or coarseness of its reticulations.

> B. Growing or multiplying the number of struts or crossovers.

> C. Mimicking the surfaces of, for example, conventional structures into or onto which it is projected.

> D. Changing by degrees the type of infill or skinning that it carries.

BUCHAREST 2000

Despite the passing of Romania'a totalitarian regime, visible and invisible scars deface the center of the capital city. The singular and violent nature of this transition, along with the built legacy of the Ceausescu regime (an inflated monumental urbansim), enables the persistence of structures of meaning that in the context of the postindustrial West belong to an almost forgotten time. The eagerly awaited reflowering of the material and cultural life of Bucharest is inevitably attended by monuments to recent tyranny.

Proposals, therefore, that attempt to restore the pre-1980s fabric, or conversely, those that propose a radical elimination of the 1980–89 Ceaucescu projects would, in their respective ways, engage in utopian models that are wholly inadequate to the situation at hand. The former indulges in a nostalgia for a lost city—a city that in any case is so rent by the 1980–89 intervention that no amount of local restoration could repair the wound or take into account the unprecedented planning demands presented by probable future socioeconomic realities. The latter, while obviously unrealistic in terms of economics (it is unlikely that the city will be inclined to demolish the Ceaucescu projects), is unfounded in perhaps more profound ways. Elimination of these monuments amounts to a totalitarian gesture in itself (whatever the style of its replacement), for it suppresses a history that is still very much alive and for that reason still very much a threat.

What is torn—torn must remain.
—Ludwig Wittgenstein

Rather than attempt to replicate an erased fabric, our proposal seeks to invigorate central Bucharest through a series of infrastructural grafts that, while responsive to the existing context (none of the buildings of the 1980s intervention will be touched), inherently produce their own patterns of growth.

The highway—an access that is not an axis.

Our plan endorses the production of new urban morphologies that would locate themselves at the zones of systematic conflict between a proposed high-speed vehicular loop and the contexts it crosses. The loop traverses the length of the axis of the People's Palace—effectively linking areas laid waste by the 1980s interventions. More important, it will serve to revalue the totalitarian effects of the axis through a two fold process: first, by impoverishing its symbolic trajectory with the "lateralizing" capacities of the highway (along with large systems-derived programs, such as shopping malls); and, second, by tempering the brutality of the highway by burying it under a mounded park that will run the entire length of the axis. Thus the axial mounded park will counter the totalitarian condition of the axis in two ways: through the landform that continuously deflects paths and views away from the axis; and through the intimate landscape created that promotes strolling and small-group interaction over forced parades.

The success of the proposal hinges on the capacity of these morphologies to actively mediate between global systems of transport and exchange and a specific site in the city. The morphologies must therefore, necessarily, derive from and be affiliated with the global (highway) system, yet be responsive to the context. In this sense they are globally rather than contextually driven.

The revitalization of Bucharest depends on the powerful forces of cultural and economic transformation engendered by a cosmopolitanizing infrastructure rather than by a provincial contextualism.

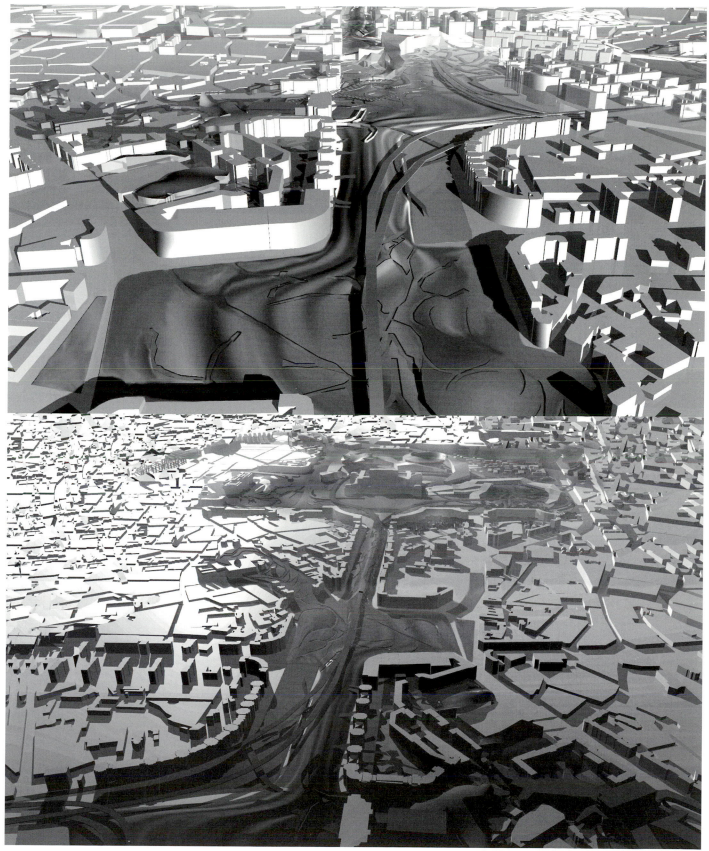

Bucharest 2000, Romania, 1996. Views of model.

Bucharest 2000. View of model.

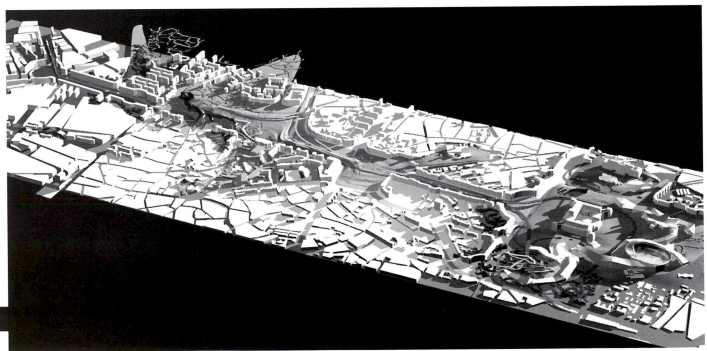

Bucharest 2000. View of model.

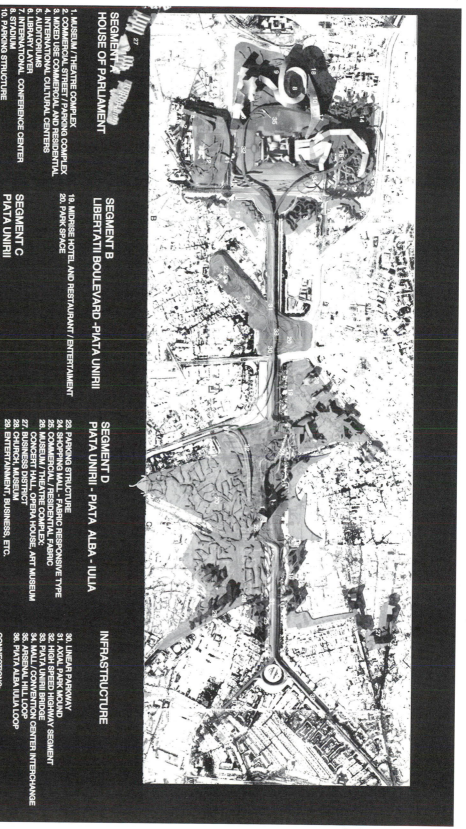

SEGMENT A
HOUSE OF PARLIAMENT

1. MUSEUM / THEATRE COMPLEX
2. COMMERCIAL STREET / PARKING COMPLEX
3. MIXED USE COMMERCIAL AND RESIDENTIAL
4. INTERNATIONAL CULTURAL CENTERS
5. AUDITORIUMS
6. LIBRARY LAYER
7. INTERNATIONAL CONFERENCE CENTER
8. STADIUM
9. PARKING STRUCTURE
10. CONVENTION CENTER, EXHIBITION HALLS

SEGMENT B
LIBERTATII BOULEVARD -PIATA UNIRII

19. MIDRISE HOTEL AND RESTAURANT / ENTERTAINMENT
20. PARK SPACE

SEGMENT C
PIATA UNIRII

SEGMENT D
PIATA UNIRII - PIATA ALBA - IULIA

23. PARKING STRUCTURE
24. SHOPPING MALL - FABRIC RESPONSIVE TYPE
25. COMMERCIAL / RESIDENTIAL FABRIC
26. MUSEUM / THEATRE COMPLEX:
    CONCERT HALL, OPERA HOUSE, ART MUSEUM
27. BUSINESS DISTRICT
28. CHURCH, MUSEUM
29. ENTERTAINMENT, BUSINESS, ETC.

INFRASTRUCTURE

30. LINEAR PARKWAY
31. AXIAL PARK MOUND
32. HIGH SPEED HIGHWAY SEGMENT
33. PIATA UNIRII BRIDGE
34. MALL / CONVENTION CENTER INTERCHANGE
35. ARSENAL HILL LOOP
36. PIATA ALBA IULIA LOOP

CONNECTIONS:

Bucharest 2000. site plan

169

YOKOHAMA PORT TERMINAL

Concept

Our proposal was formulated in response to what we perceived as the inherent dichotomy between global systems of transport and exchange and the condition of the specific sites at which the systems intersect. Such conditions are exemplified by the port of Yokohama and specifically encoded within the program of the port terminal proper. The recognition of this liminal condition prompted us to recognize that our proposal should seek to encompass the general functional imperatives of the cruise terminal (as a smoothly functioning link between land and water transport) and the specific civic possibilities suggested by the pier configuration itself. Following from this, our proposal was conceived as an incomplete or partial building — partial, both conceptually and formally, in recognition of the fact that such programs frame thresholds in two distinct yet overlapping continuums: in the cycle of embarkation and disembarkation of the cruise terminal; and at the civic level as a place of rest and recreation in the course of an excursion. Consequently, completion, both physically and virtually, is effected only periodically: in the linkage of terminal to cruise ship or in the closure of the completed urban event.

Structure

The proposed terminal is a shed building measuring 412 meters in length and composed of 27 three-hinged, steel trussed arches of 42.5 meters average span placed at 16-meter intervals. These arches are joined longitudinally by trussed members of conventional configuration and purlins carrying either metal cladding or the extensive glazing envisioned for the project. The steel shed structure springs from hinges placed at the surface of the main level. The hinges are carried on concrete piers extending from the basement parking level through the apron to the surface of the main level. Horizontal thrust from the arches is counteracted by tension rods connecting opposing arch hinges. These tension rods also serve as partial support for the main-floor slab.

This large shed, though affiliated with its nineteenth-century antecedents, differs in the sense that while the nineteenth-century types were characterized by a totalizing conception employing uniform and repetitive structural units enclosing a single homogeneous space, this proposal engenders heterogeneity through selective perturbations and extensions of the structural frames. The transformation yields a complex of spaces that smoothly incorporate the multiple terminal, civic and garden programs within and below its span.

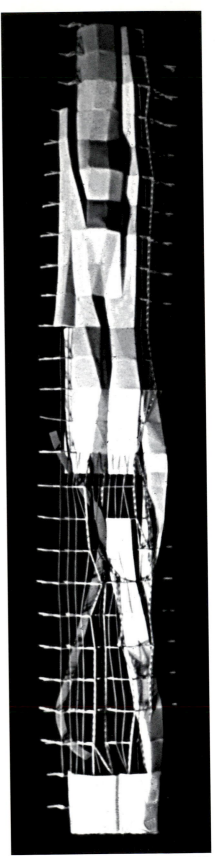

Yokohama Port Terminal, Japan, 1994.

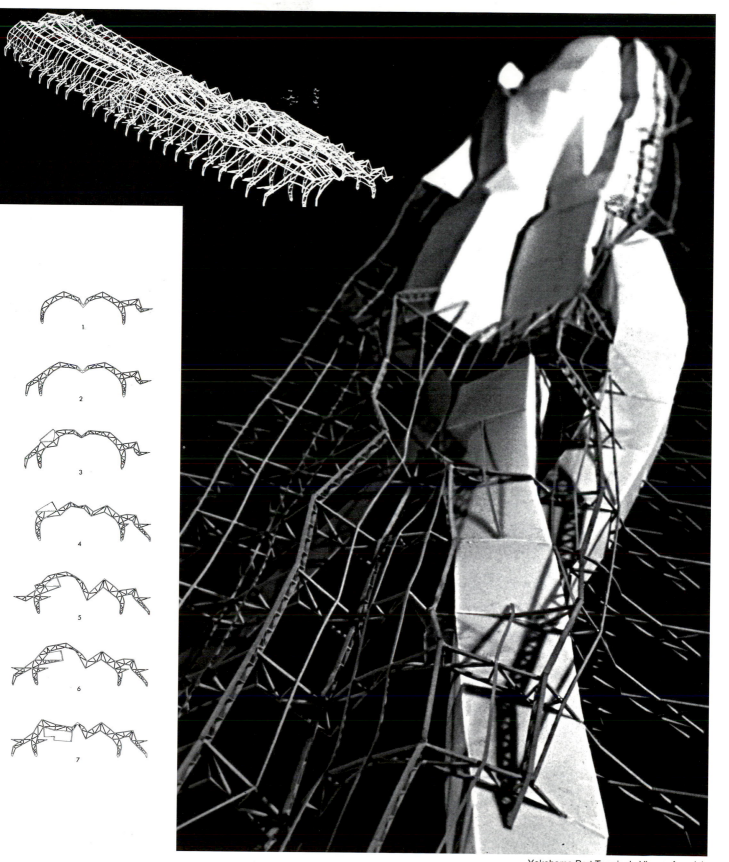

Yokohama Port Terminal. Views of model.

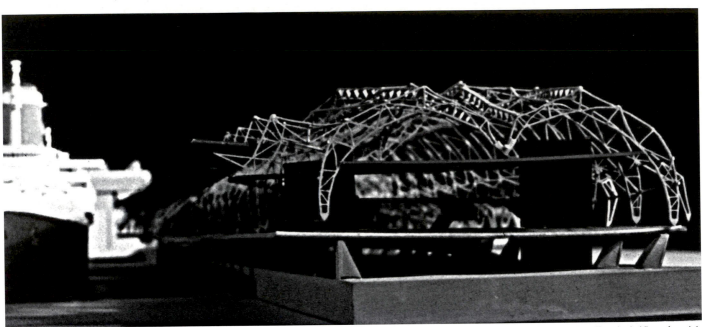

Yokohama Port Terminal. View of model.

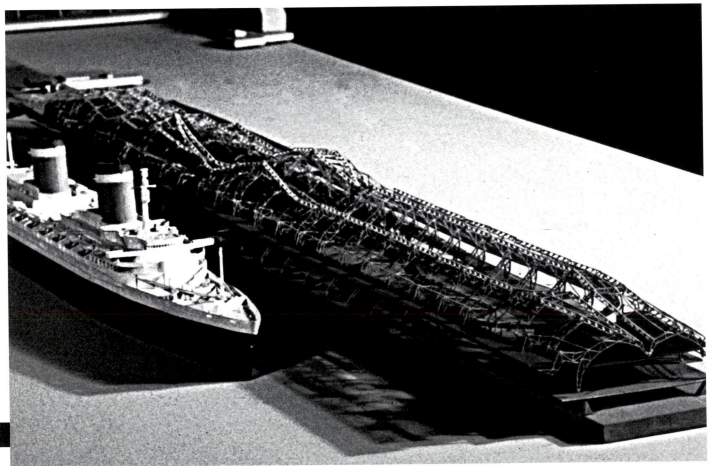

172

Yokohama Port Terminal. View of model.

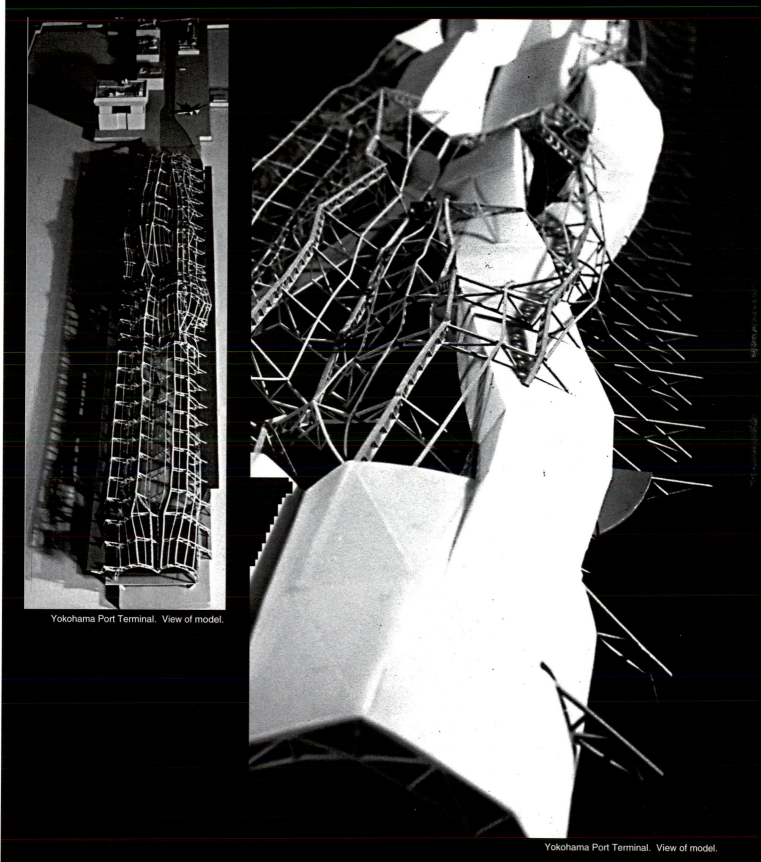

Yokohama Port Terminal. View of model.

Yokohama Port Terminal. View of model.

Yokohama Port Terminal. View of model.

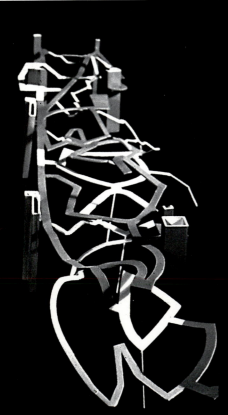

174

Yokohama Port Terminal. Circulation.

Yokohama Port Terminal. View of model.

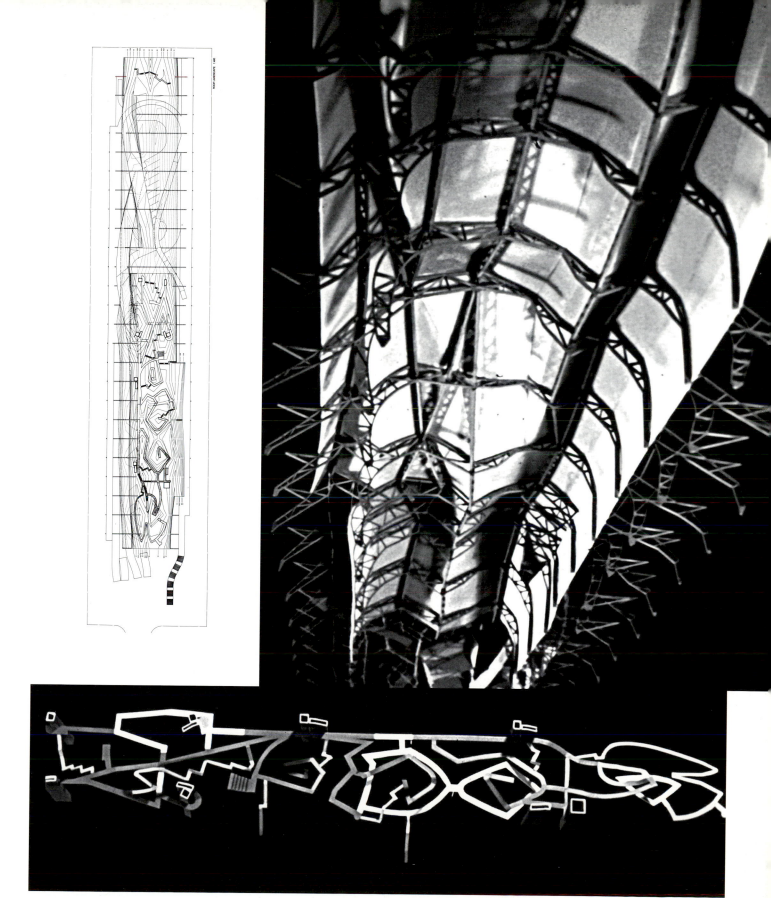

Top: Yokohama Port Terminal. View of model. *Bottom:* Yokohama Port Terminal. Circulation.

KANSAI LIBRARY

General Approach

Our proposal for the Kansai (Japan) branch of the National Diet Library seeks to address the apparent paradox surrounding the universal proliferation of data, the presumed placelessness of information and the persistent necessity, nevertheless, of finding a definition for this condition in architecture. Beyond the admittedly important legal and archival need to preserve hard copies of documents, the persistence of the library may be ascribed to less recognized processes attendant on globalization. The general decentralization and dispersion of institutions made possible by new technologies overshadow a correspondingly specific trend toward centrality and agglomeration both within and appended to major urban centers in global economies. Japan's principal cities (where most of the country's data is produced and consumed) have seen the advent of information zones: developments consisting of buildings and public spaces relatively small in scale, whose organization promotes mutual interests and information exchange through direct communication. A new form of public space thus arises out of the interaction of two logics: first, the close proximity of major institutions and corporations, and second, the consequent influx of smaller institutions and services that are sustained by the presence of their larger neighbors. The success of such co-dependent organizations is predicated not simply on the major institutions that initiate the information zone but also on their capacity to act as catalysts for the advent of new programs and uses. Our proposal, therefore, embodies two distinct yet related imperatives: to fulfill the explicit programmatic criteria of the library, and develop implicit spatialities that would foster the new and unforeseen irruptions of program brought about by the "information zone."

Stack Building

The Stack Building consists of a bar measuring 182 meters in length, 25 meters in width and 25 meters in height. It is made up of steel-truss walls, oriented vertically, which act as gigantic storage units for automated, compact and fixed stacks. Books and documents are accessed via catwalks and an automated conveyor system that efficiently routes library materials to and from the reading rooms or shipping and receiving departments. Since the Stack Building is organized around the concept of the storage wall, stacks are categorized sectionally in layers. There are no horizontal slabs or floors as such. Horizontal movement is accomplished along catwalks and the automated conveyor system. Between the storage walls are narrow open wells extending from ground to roof that allow filtered natural illumination to enter the entire section of the building through skylights.

Public Spaces

The Library Building, which measures 220 meters by 55 meters, is composed of three ramped slabs. The slabs are formed so as to maximize continuity and multiple interconnections among the public spaces and levels. Topological deformations—cuts, mounds, ramps, ripples and stairs—render the library a programmed landscape that has the capacity not only to ensure the smooth functioning of the major programs but also to foster the emergence of new and unanticipated configurations of social space. The visitors' entry into the library is from two locations. Pedestrians and visitors arriving by bus gain access via the pedestrian road located at the front of the building. A ramp leads up to the second level and joins the drop-off area in front of the main entrance. Entry into the lobby is also available from the parking level via ramps. The lobby space provides direct entry into the restaurant, store, lockers and auditorium above. Controlled access into the main reading room is possible through five ramps that lead to a reading room above. Programming in the library is based on the notion of precincts rather than dividing walls. Consequently, the main reading room programs bleed into both the floor below and the Asian Document and Information Center farther up the ramp.

Structure and Resistance to Lateral Forces

The two-way prestressed slabs of the Library Building are suspended from a prestressed steel roof of six meters maximum depth by a nine-meter grid of suspension cables five centimeters in diameter, passing through the ramped slabs. The roof is carried on four steel piers. The large plan dimension of the slabs and roof necessitate distinct responses to lateral—thermal, seismic and wind forces. Each concrete slab is divided in two across the long dimension by a thermal expansion joint with mechanical dampers designed to absorb any lateral dynamic movement. Since the prestressed steel roof must remain monolithic in order to support the slabs below, expansion from solar gain becomes considerable. The roof safely transmits this movement to its four piers, two of which are fixed to footings; the opposing pair are allowed to slide freely on Teflon pads. The perimeter of the entire Library Building is enclosed by a lattice truss of 20-centimeter welded steel tubes. The ramp/roof assembly thus forms a rigid box that provides resistance to possible lateral earthquake forces. Vertical seismic movement is also effectively damped by the relative flexibility of roof and slab assemblies.

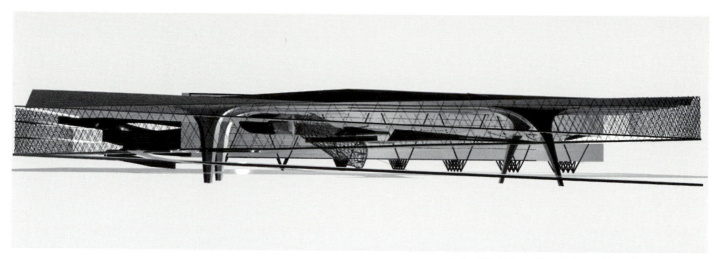

National Diet Library, Kansai, Japan, 1996. Exterior elevation.

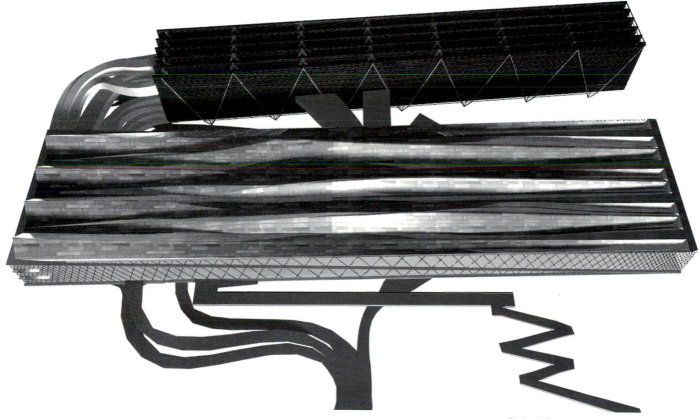

National Diet Library, Kansai. View of model.

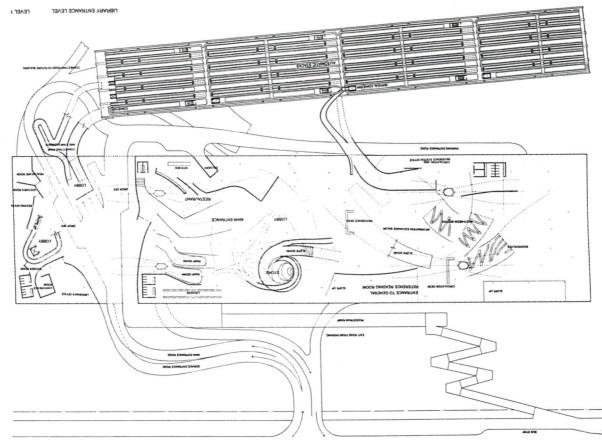

National Diet Library, Kansai. Entrance level plan.

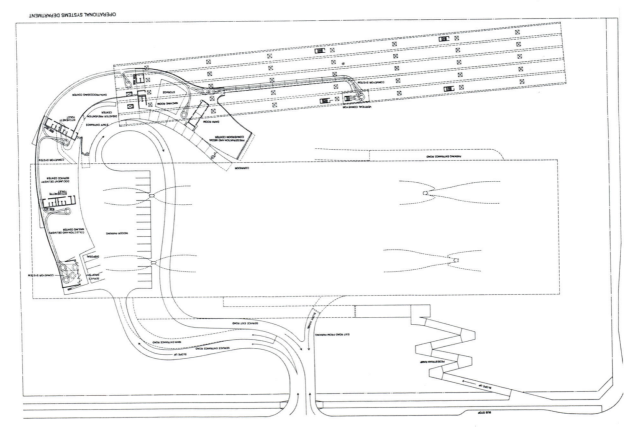

National Diet Library. Operational systems department.

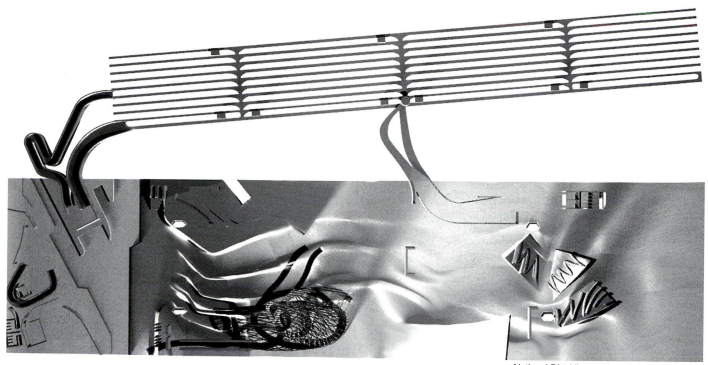

National Diet Library, Kansai. View of model.

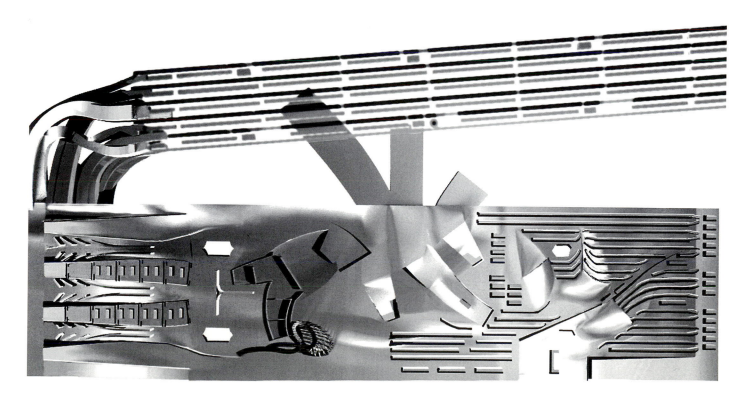

National Diet Library, Kansai. View of model.

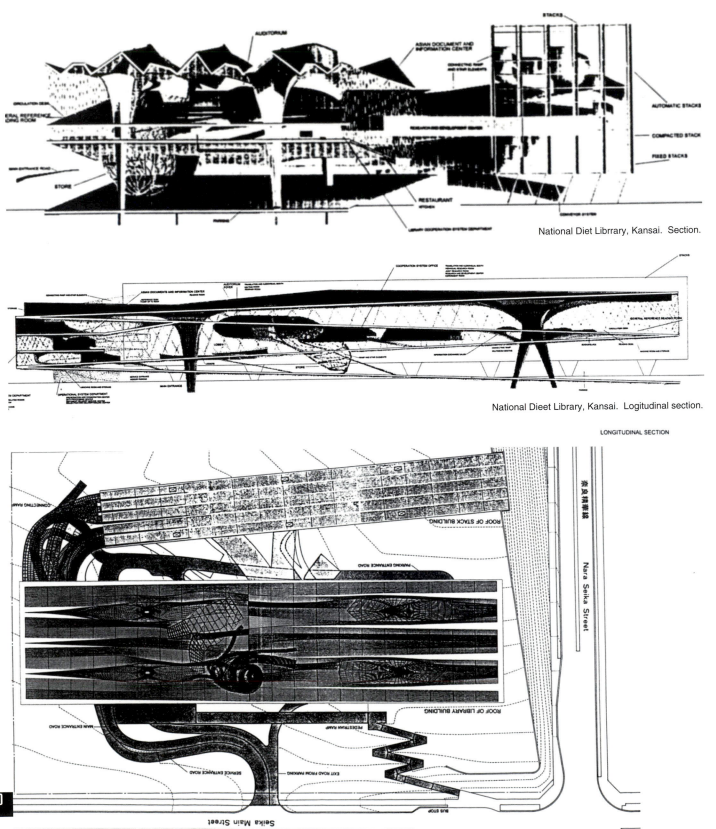

National Diet Librrary, Kansai. Section.

National Dieet Library, Kansai. Logitudinal section.

LONGITUDINAL SECTION

奈良精華線

Nara Seika Street

ROOF OF STACK BUILDING

CONNECTING RAMP

PARKING ENTRANCE ROAD

ROOF OF LIBRARY BUILDING

MAIN ENTRANCE ROAD

PEDESTRIAN RAMP

SERVICE ENTRANCE ROAD

EXIT ROAD FROM PARKING

BUS STOP

Seika Main Street

National Diet Library, Kansai. Site plan.

National Diet Library, Kansai. View of model.

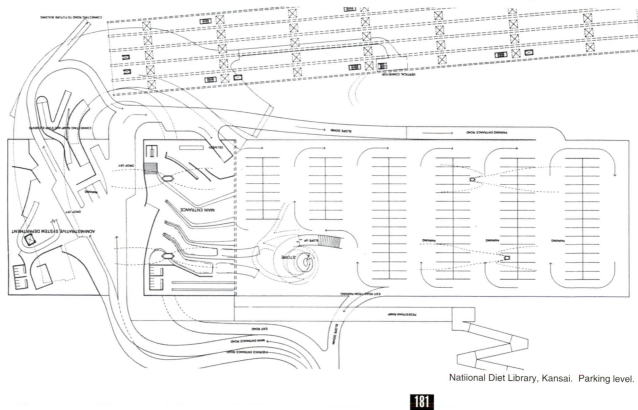

Natiional Diet Library, Kansai. Parking level.

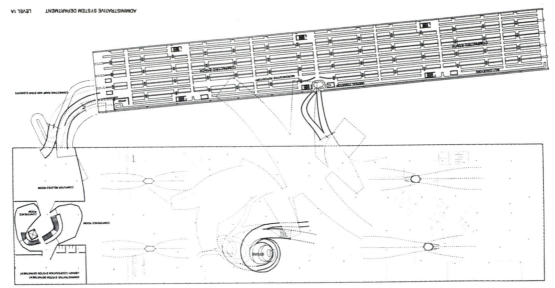

National Diet Library, Kansai. Third level.

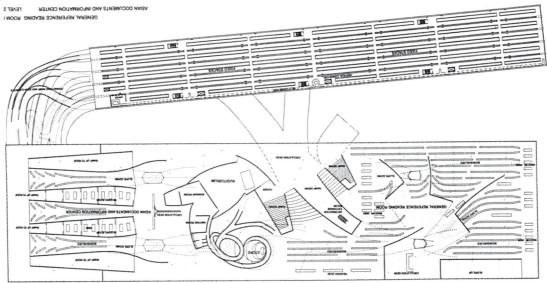

National Diet Library, Kansai. Second level.

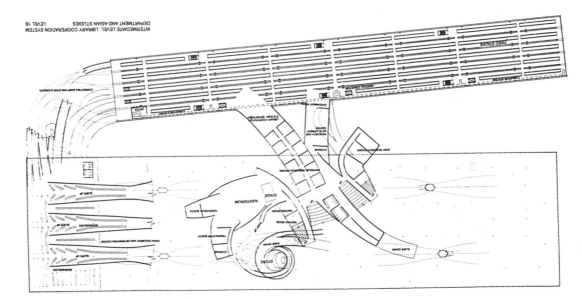

National Diet Library, Kansai. First level.

National Diet Library, Kansai. View of model.

National Diet Library, Kansai. View of model.

The work presented in this article was on view at Columbia University's South Gallery, Buell Hall from October 13 to November 18, 1995.

Jesse Reiser is a fellow of the American Academy in Rome and adjunct assistant professor of architecture at Columbia University.

Nanako Umemoto was formerly adjunct assistant professor of urban design at Osaka University of Art and is assistant professor of architecture at Columbia University.

Notes

1. Paul Valéry, "The Intellectual Crisis," *Selected Writings of Paul Valéry* (New York: New Directions, 1950), 118.

2. This is a paraphrase of a description of the acoustic conception of the Orange County Performing Arts Center theater by the Blurock Partnership and Caudill-Rowlett-Scott, Associated Architects. Our proposal "notionally joins" three shoebox halls instead of the two in the CRS design. See Michael Forsyth, *Auditoria* (New York: Van Nostrand Reinhold, 1987), 73.

3. Cf. Greg Lynn, "Architectural Curvilinearity: The Folded, the Pliant and the Supple," *Architectural Design* 102. *Folding in Architecture* (1993): 8–15.

4. The terms "geodetic" and "geodesic" are technically interchangeable; we will distinguish the "supple" employment from the modernist one (like Fuller's) by letting Barnes Wallis's term, "geodetics," stand for the former.

5. William Green, *Famous Bombers of the Second World War,* vol. 1 (London: MacDonald Press, 1959).

6. D'Arcy Wentworth Thompson, *On Growth and Form* (New York: Dover, 1992), 675–76.

7. Martin Bowman, *Wellington, the Geodetic Giant* (Shrewsbury: Airlife, 1989), 3–5.

8. *Monocoque,* from the Greek *monos* and the French *coque,* meaning "single shell." In the pure monocoque structure, there is no internal bracing; the shell bears all the loads. A semimonocoque design, which has stiffeners running the length of the fusilage, is also referred to by engineers as a stressed-skin construction.

CONTENTS   VOL. ONE

Jacques Derrida: Invitation to a Discussion

Elizabeth Diller/Ricardo Scofidio: reViewing

Sylviane Agacinski: Shares of Invention

Peter Rice: Unstable Structures

Mark Wigley: Heidegger's House—The Violence of the Domestic

**Giovanna Borradori: The Italian Heidegger—Philosophy, Architecture
                       and Weak Thought**

Kazuo Shinohara: The New Machine—Absorbing Chaos

Geoffrey Bennington: After the Event

John Rajchman: Weakness, Technologies, Events (An Introduction)

Afterwords: Architecture and Theory Conference

CONTENTS   VOL. TWO

John Hejduk: Oslo Fall Night

Wiel Arets: An Alabaster Skin

**Jean Baudrillard: The Timisoara Syndrome—The Télécratie
                    and the Revolution**

Bernard Tschumi: Six Concepts

Peter Eisenman: Folding in Time—The Singularity of Rebstock

Catherine Ingraham: Moving Target

Paul Virilio: The Law of Proximity

**Félix Guattari: Space and Corporeity
                  Memorial text by John Rajchman**

CONTENTS VOL. THREE

Saskia Sassen: Analytic Borderlands—Economy and Culture in the Global City

Rem Koolhaas: Urban Operations

Peter Marcuse: Density and Social Justice—Is There a Relationship? A Historical Examination

Stan Allen: Its Exercise, Under Certain Conditions

Stanislaus von Moos: Le Corbusier, the Monument and the Metropolis

Itsuko Hasegawa: Architecture as Another Nature

Robin Evans: Le Corbusier and the Sexual Identity of Architecture Memorial text by Mark Rakatansky

CONTENTS VOL. FOUR

Jacques Herzog: Recent Work of Herzog & de Meuron

Steven Holl: Pre-theoretical Ground

Architecture Culture 1943–1968: A Round-table Discussion Joan Ockman, Alan Colquhoun, Jacques Gubler, Jean-Louis Cohen

Kenneth Frampton: Toward an Urban Landscape

Arata Isozaki: PROJECTS: 1983–1990

Hans Hollein: PROJECTS: 1960–1991

Andrew Benjamin: Event, Time, Repetition

Elliot Feingold: Seminar on Technology, Humanism and Space

CONTENTS VOL. FIVE

Mark Taylor: Seaming

Hani Rashid: Ceci n'est pas un Building

K. Michael Hays: Hannes Meyer and the Production of Effects

Nasrine Seraji: The Event of Space

Beatriz Colomina: Mies Not

Toyo Ito: Floating Pao in the Stream

Chizuko Ueno: Urbansim and the Transformation
of Sexuality: Edo to Tokyo

Joseph Abram: Hugo Herdeg and the World of Objects:
The Space-time of Photography— Ready-made,
Zero Point and Picnolepsy

assemblage

A Critical Journal of Architecture and Design Culture

An advanced journal of architectural theory and criticism, **Assemblage** seriously and thoughtfully appraises contemporary practice. Provocative, polemical, and exploratory, **Assemblage** examines the relationships between culture and design, and between theory and material reality. Each extensively illustrated issue presents essays, projects, and debates by leading and emerging scholars, theorists, and practitioners. Work is drawn from a wide range of fields: architectural and art history and theory, cultural criticism, literary theory, philosophy, and politics.

1996 subscription prices: Individual $60 / Institution $122 / Student* & Retired $38 *Copy of current ID required. Outside U.S.A. add $16 shipping. Canadians also add 7% GST. Prepayment is required. Send check—drawn against a U.S. bank in U.S. funds, payable to *Assemblage*—MC, AMEX or VISA number to: MIT Press Journals, 55 Hayward Street, Cambridge, MA 02142 Tel: 617-253-2889 Fax: 617-577-1545 journals-orders@mit.edu Three times a year April/August/ December 112 pp. per issue, 8 3/8 x 10 1/4, illustrated ISSN 0889-3012 Published by The MIT Press. Prices are subject to change without notice.

k. michael hays

catherine ingraham

alicia kennedy

editors